U0111246

**A Study on the Emergency Legislative Power of
the Chief Executive of Hong Kong SAR**

Based on the analysis of the text of
the Emergency Regulations Ordinance

香港特區行政長官
的緊急立法權研究

基於對《緊急情況規例條例》文本的分析

朱世海　黃海鵬　　著

目錄

前言

為了填補香港現有法律制度的漏洞，使香港能夠與尚無長期司法協助安排的司法管轄區展開個案合作，香港特別行政區政府（以下簡稱“香港特區政府”）於 2019 年 4 月向香港特別行政區立法會提交了《2019 年逃犯及刑事事宜相互法律協助法例（修訂）條例草案》（以下簡稱《逃犯條例》）。自 2019 年 6 月開始，香港的部分反對派和一些激進勢力不斷藉和平遊行集會之名，進行各種各樣激進的抗爭活動，反對立法會通過《逃犯條例》。2019 年 10 月 23 日，香港立法會召開會議，保安局局長宣佈撤回《逃犯條例》修訂草案。然而，香港街頭的激進抗爭活動並沒有停止，反而升級為暴亂。大量暴徒無視法律，以蒙面的方式繼續變本加厲地實施暴力破壞，導致香港許多銀行、店鋪、商場、學校以及地鐵等設施被打砸搶燒，破壞程度十分嚴重，香港亦因此連續幾日幾乎陷入"全城混亂"和"全城癱瘓"的危險狀態。為了儘快平息暴亂、重建香港法治權威和依法恢復社會秩序，2019 年 10 月 4 日，時任香港特別行政區行政長官（以下簡稱"香港特區行政長官"）林鄭月娥對外宣佈，她已經會同行政會議作出了決定，依據《緊急情況規例條例》（以下簡稱《緊急條例》）第 1 條在"危害公安"情況下可訂立附屬法規的規定，根據香港目前社會暴亂不斷的形勢訂立《禁止蒙面規例》，該規例於 2019 年 10 月 5 日實施。

香港特區行政長官依據《緊急條例》訂立《禁止蒙面規例》，在香港受到很多質疑和批評，即使建制派內部當時亦有主張不宜依據條文內容粗陋的《緊急條例》制定《禁止蒙面規例》。有些香港人士認為行政長官依據《緊急條例》訂立《禁止蒙面規例》違反《香港特別行政區基本法》（以下簡稱《香港基本法》），亦有一些立法會議員向香港特別行政區高等法院（以下簡稱"香港特區高等法院"）提出訴訟，請求法院裁判行政長官依據《緊急條例》訂定《禁止蒙面規例》違"憲"（"憲"指《香港基本法》，下同），香港特區高等法院原訟庭支持了原告的訴求。香港特區政府向高等法院上訴庭提起上訴，上訴庭推翻一審裁判，判定行政長官依據《緊急條例》訂定《禁止蒙面規例》合

"憲"，該裁判意見亦得到香港特別行政區終審法院（以下簡稱"香港特區終審法院"）的支持。儘管行政長官會同行政會議根據《緊急條例》訂立《禁止蒙面規例》合"憲"，但這並不意味著《緊急條例》本身不存在問題。因為該條例制定於一百年前，存在明顯的缺陷，應及時加以完善。

本書首章探討緊急立法權的一般理論。一般說來，緊急權力的行使需要立法、行政和司法三方聯動，涉及三種權力的配合。緊急立法權的構成包括實體要件和程序要件。緊急立法權具有從屬性、有限性和靈活性的特徵。緊急立法權的權力結構包括縱向權力結構和橫向權力結構兩個方面。緊急立法權的功能包括維護國家等共同體生存的必要手段、恢復正常憲法秩序的法律保障等內容。緊急立法權應具有合理性、合法性和正當性。而對於緊急立法權是否合理，筆者將從感性和理性兩個方面加以分析。緊急立法權的合法性，體現為具有現實的法律依據並受到監督制約。緊急立法權的正當性，要求緊急立法權的實施必須符合該國的憲法。

第二章分析香港特區行政長官緊急立法權的學理。香港特區行政長官緊急立法權的憲制依據是港英立法局在 1922 年通過的《緊急條例》。當香港於 1997 年回歸中國時，《緊急條例》與許多其他原有法律一樣，成為香港特別行政區法律制度的一個組成部分。香港特區行政長官緊急立法權所指的"緊急"是指《緊急條例》規定的"緊急情況"和"危害公安"。緊急立法是附屬立法、附屬法例或附屬法規，但這種附屬立法與一般附屬立法存在重大區別——行政長官立法的自主性很高，不是對立法會立法的具體化，而是可以根據《緊急條例》的授權制定全新的規範，可將此稱為"獨立附屬立法"。香港特區行政長官緊急立法權，除了具有緊急立法的一般功能外，還具有填補法制漏洞、豐富應急措施和拓展彈性空間等特別功能。

第三章探討香港特區行政長官緊急立法權與香港政治體制的關係。香港特別行政區政治體制無疑屬於行政主導，同時亦具有權力分立的特徵，兩者高度統一於香港特別行政區政治體制之中。香港的行政主導體制有一定的歷史淵源，回歸前的政治體制亦可以稱為"行政主導體制"，但那時的"行政主導體制"是專制體制，與回歸後的行政主導體制存在根本區別。回歸後的行政主導體制包含權力分立的元素，是一種民主體制。香港特別行政區政治體制的設計者，就是要賦予行政長官較多的權力，以使行政長官及其領導政府的權力相對於立法會的權力處於優勢地位。因此，《緊急條例》賦予行政長官緊急立法權符合《香港基本法》的立法原意。行政長官的緊急立法權滿足應對緊急情況的需要，是香港保持穩定繁榮之必須。

第四章對香港特區《緊急條例》的合"憲"性進行判辨。《緊急條例》是符合《香港基本法》的，表現如下：其一，《緊急條例》授權行政長官會同行政會議制定緊急法具有合"憲"性；其二，行政長官的緊急立法設定刑事處罰具有合"憲"性；其三，行政長官的緊急立法修改立法會立法亦具有合"憲"性。《緊急條例》並沒有被《香港人權法案條例》或《公民權利和政治權利國際公約》廢止，仍具有效力。香港特別行政區法院（以下簡稱"香港特區法院"）無權裁判《緊急條例》是否合乎《香港基本法》，因為全國人民代表大會常務委員會事先已經確認該條例符合《香港基本法》，全國人民代表大會常務委員會的權威不容挑戰。然而，我們不能因此否定香港特區法院對於香港特區立法會立法中僅涉及自治事項條款的審查權，這不僅是實施"一國兩制"的需要，而且是落實《香港基本法》所建構起的法制秩序的需要。

第五章對香港特區《緊急條例》的缺陷進行總結。《緊急條例》是在一百年前制定的，自身難免存在缺陷。鑒於香港與英國都屬於普通法地區，而且英國的《國民緊急應變法（2004）》較為完善，故以英國的《國民緊急應變法（2004）》作為比較對象。通過從文本結構、"緊急狀態"

的定義、緊急權行使程序、權利保護和權力制約五個方面的比較，發現香港特區《緊急條例》確實存在一些缺陷。例如，《緊急條例》的文本內容顯得非常簡單粗陋、《緊急條例》規定的緊急權程序要件缺失，等等。

第六章闡述完善《緊急條例》的建議。完善《緊急條例》的首要工作，是規制香港特區行政長官緊急立法權。對行政長官緊急立法權的規制應堅持的原則有：必要性原則、比例原則、權利保留原則、資訊公開原則、程序正當原則。對香港特區行政長官的緊急立法權需要從實體和程序兩個方面加以規制。借鑒英國《國民緊急應變法（2004）》來完善香港特區《緊急條例》，應列明緊急法對相對人權利保障的具體可行措施，規範以行政長官為主導的緊急權，以及完善《緊急條例》文本。

本書是作者在所承擔的中央某機關委託課題成果基礎上擴寫而成，感謝課題成果外審專家對課題文稿品質的充分肯定及提出的寶貴修改意見。感謝香港三聯書店蘇健偉先生為編輯本書所付出的辛勞。作者希望此項研究成果能夠為香港特區《緊急條例》的完善提供些許參考，若能，也算為香港法治的發展盡了綿薄之力。當然，因作者力有不逮，此研究成果一定存在這樣或那樣的問題，還懇請方家不吝賜教。

第一章

緊急立法權的一般理論

緊急權分為緊急權利和緊急權力。前者是"公民在缺乏公力救濟途經的急迫情況下，以損害人的某一法益為代價來保護另一法益的權利"[1]。後者是指公權力機關（通常是行政機關）為應對戰爭、暴亂、自然災害、疾病等緊急情況，而享有的臨時克減公民權利和自由的權力。在世界各國的憲法中，儘管對緊急權力作出了一定的規定，但在其名稱、行使的相應實體和程序上並無統一的規定，各國"緊急"的立法形式各異。緊急立法權和一般立法權是同一立法權在不同情形下的表現形式，其本質都是國家立法權，但其行使的主體、內容、權力來源、權力範圍以及立法程序卻有很大的區別。緊急立法權的最大特點就是改變

1　陳璿：《緊急權體系建構與基本原理》，北京：北京大學出版社 2021 年版，第 1 頁。

正常狀態下的憲法關係，因為在緊急狀態下，緊急立法權主體有權通過立法或頒佈緊急命令的形式減少國家機構在正常狀態下本應承擔的憲法和法律義務，而這些憲法和法律義務主要涉及對一些公民基本權利的保護。

第一節　緊急立法權釋義

　　各國憲法對"緊急"的表述不同，"緊急法"的形式亦各異。立法權的內容豐富和複雜，一般都是由數個國家機關分工行使。一般說來，國家緊急權力的行使需要立法、行政和司法三方聯動，涉及三種權力的配合。緊急立法權的構成包括實體要件和程序要件。緊急立法權具有從屬性、有限性和靈活性的特徵。

一、緊急立法權核心詞語解讀

（一）緊急

1. 各國憲法對"緊急"的表述不同

　　目前，世界各國的憲法中對"緊急"一詞的定義存在差異，在文字表述方面也不一樣，大致有以下十一種提法：[1]

　　（1）非常情況

---

[1]　各國憲法對"緊急"的不同表述可參見徐高、莫紀宏：《外國緊急狀態法律制度》，北京：法律出版社1994年版，第1-2頁；郭春明：《緊急狀態法律制度研究》，北京：中國檢察出版社2004年版，第5-6頁；王旭坤：《緊急不避法治》，北京：法律出版社2009年版，第14-15頁。

1975 年《希臘共和國憲法》第 44 條第 1 款規定，在刻不容緩和無法預見的非常情況下，共和國總統，應內閣的請求，得頒佈立法性法令。

（2）戒嚴狀態

1987 年《菲律賓共和國憲法》第 7 章第 18 條第 1 款規定，在遇到侵略或叛亂時，總統得應公共安全的需要而在不超過六十天的時期內停止施行人身保護令特權，或在菲律賓全國或任一地區實施戒嚴令。在宣佈戒嚴狀態或停止施行人身保護令特權的四十八小時內，總統應親自或書面報告國會。

（3）緊急命令

1979 年《孟加拉國人民共和國憲法》第 5 章第 95 條第 1 款規定，在議會解散或閉會期間，如果總統認為存在必須採取緊急措施的形勢，得制定和頒佈他／她認為必要的緊急命令，緊急命令自頒佈之日起具有如同議會法令的法律效力。

（4）特殊情況

1947 年《意大利共和國憲法》第 13 條第 3 款規定，在法律有明確規定的緊急需要的特殊情況下，警察機關可以採取臨時措施。

（5）防禦狀態

原聯邦德國在 1968 年通過的《基本法的第 17 次改
法》第 10 章（甲）就是對防禦狀態的規定。

（6）緊急事件

1961 年《委內瑞拉共和國憲法》規定，遇到緊急事
件，可能擾亂共和國和平的混亂，或者影響經濟和社會生
活的嚴重情況的時候，共和國總統可以限制或停止憲法的
保證或者某一些保證。

（7）緊急情況

1971 年《阿拉伯聯合酋長國臨時憲法》第 113 條規
定，在最高委員會閉會期間，如因刻不容緩的緊急情況，
必須立即頒佈聯邦法律，聯邦總統和部長會議可以法令形
式共同頒佈具有法律效力的必要的法律，但其內容不得和
本憲法的規定相抵觸。

（8）非常狀態

1971 年《保加利亞人民共和國憲法》第 94 條規定，
國務委員會在國民議會閉會期間可宣佈非常狀態。

（9）緊急赦令

1978 年《泰王國憲法》第 157 條規定，如為維護國
家安全、公共安全、國家經濟穩定或抗災搶險等刻不容緩
的緊急需要，國王得頒佈具有法律效力的緊急赦令。

（10）軍法管制

1971 年《阿拉伯聯合酋長國臨時憲法》第 146 條規定，如有必要，按法律規定，根據聯邦總統建議，經聯邦部長會議和最高委員會同意，由聯邦總統下令宣佈實行軍法管制。

（11）戰爭狀態和戒嚴

1982 年《中華人民共和國憲法》（以下簡稱《中國憲法》）第 67 條規定了全國人民代表大會常務委員會的職權，其中第 19 項規定，在全國人民代表大會閉會期間，如果遇到國家遭受武裝侵犯或者必須履行國際間共同防止侵略的條約的情況，決定戰爭狀態的宣佈；第 20 項規定，決定全國或者個別省、自治區、直轄市的戒嚴。在 2004 年，"戒嚴"被修改為"緊急狀態"。

由以上可見，很多國家的成文憲法儘管都對緊急權力作出了一定的規定，但在緊急權力名稱、行使的相應實體和程序上並無統一的規定。

2. 各國"緊急法"的形式各異

隨著各國對緊急狀態立法的重視，國際上緊急立法的數量越來越多，可以按照不同的標準進行分類。比如按照立法效力層級的不同，大致可以分為四類：在憲法中規定、在應對突發性重大自然災害的立法中規定、在專門的緊急法中規定和在其他立法形式中規定。[1]另外，根據立法內容的不同，大致可以分為以下三類：

（1）軍事管制或戒嚴法

最初，緊急狀態的立法主要是針對戰爭、政變、動亂等危及國家安全的情況，國家通過實行軍事管制或戒嚴等手段來應對危機，如俄國的《俄羅斯聯邦戰時狀態法》、美國的《反恐怖主義法》、韓國的《國軍組織法》，中國的《戒嚴法》。世界上還有許多國家在《國防法》、《戰爭法》、《戰爭動員令》等戰爭法規或軍事法規中規定緊急狀態制度。

（2）自然災害救助法

一些國家通過制定各種災害救助法律來規範重大災害發生時的緊急狀態應對方法、對策、技術等，規範各級政府制定對救助特種自然災害的緊急狀態制度。美國在1950年制定的《災害救助和緊急援助法》、在1977年制定的《地震災害減輕法》，就屬於此類緊急立法。日本在1947年制定的《災害救助法》、在1961年制定的《災害對策基本法》、1978年制定的《大地震對策特別措施法》、《大城市震災對策推進綱要》等，亦屬於此類緊急立法。

1　呂景勝：《〈緊急狀態法〉立法研究》，載《中國人民大學學報》2003年第5期，第107-108頁。

（3）恐怖活動、動亂治理法

如美國在 1976 年制定了《緊急狀態法》，而在"9·11"事件發生後，美國在緊急狀態的應對預案和法規方面進行了更加周密、嚴謹、細緻的修訂，使得《緊急狀態法》及其實施細則更加具有可操作性和實戰性。

（二）立法權

1. 立法權的概念

國內法學界一般都把立法權簡單定義為國家制定、修改或廢止法律的權力，但這種定義只是從立法權形式意義的角度進行界定。英國啟蒙學者洛克指出："立法權是享有權利來指導如何運用國家的力量以保障這個社會及其成員的權力"。[1] 郭道暉先生曾說："立法權概念是一個豐富的整體，具有多樣的規定性。"[2]

立法權核心內容就是創制法律的活動，通常認為屬於國家主權行為，是國家的一項重要權力。當然，獨立政治實體及香港、澳門特區這樣的主權國下的地區也具有立法權，但為表述的方便，筆者在本書中把立法權主體一般表述為國家。立法權本身包含的內容十分豐富，其定義有多

---

1 （英）洛克：《政府論》（下冊），葉啟芳、瞿菊農譯，北京：商務印書館 2004 年版，第 89 頁。

2 郭道暉：《論國家立法權》，載《中外法學》1994 年第 4 期，第 9 頁。

種分類。從制定主體的類別來劃分立法權，可以分為議會立法權和政府立法權，即立法機關立法權和行政機關立法權。從制定主體層次的角度來劃分，可以分為國家立法權和地方立法權。從立法權的內容來劃分，可以分為實體性權力和程序性權力，其中實體性權力包括制定、認可、補充、修改、廢止法規等內容，程序性權力包括提出、審議、表決、公佈、批准法規等內容。從立法權涉及的範圍來劃分，可以分為綜合立法權和單項立法權。從立法權行使的方式劃分，可以分為直接性立法權和授權性立法權。中國內地學者結合內地法律淵源，還把立法權分為廣義立法權和狹義立法權：廣義的立法權是指制定和修改憲法、法律、行政規章、地方性規章等活動，而狹義的立法權是指制定和修改憲法和法律的活動。

從上述立法權的諸多分類中可以看出，立法權的內容十分豐富和複雜，單純由一個國家機關來行使立法權不太現實，一般都是由數個國家機關分工行使。在分工行使立法權的過程中，各個國家機關的權力有所不同。其中，國家立法機關享有的立法權最廣泛，政府機關享有的立法權則次於立法機關。從當今世界各國的立法權實施情況來看，政府除了享有對立法機關立法一定程度上的提案權、公佈權和否決權，還有行政法規和行政法令的制定權、立法機關委託的立法權等。但是，由於各國的國情不同，並非各國的行政機關都享有上述種類的立法權，亦不是所有國家的全部行政機關都享有立法權。[1] 由此可見，立法權是對一個國家所有立法行動的總稱，是一種複合型和綜合型的權力，是一個國家各方面立法權的總稱。在這樣一個綜合的權力體系裏面，各機關行使立法權存在差別，但又共同維護立法權的統一和權威。

2. 立法權的行使方式

（1）立法權是國家的一項權能，其行使方式之一是使用權和所有權可以分開。[2] 單一制國家只有一個立法權，一般是由主權代表機關行使。但是，只有一個立法權不能等同於只有一個立法機關。在立法實踐中，由於立法工作的專業性、複雜性和時效性等特性，由單一的立法機關無法完成龐雜的立法工作，需要一個立法體系來協作完成，這就決定了立法工作可以由不同的機關完成。但是，從事立法活動的機關不一定擁有立法權，比如授權立法，立法的具體事項由被授權機關完成，立法權並沒有因此轉移，授權機關仍然可以收回授權。可見，立法權的所有和使用具有可分離性。複合制國家可能存在多個立法權，但是每個

1　劉恆：《論行政立法權》，載《法學評論》1995 年第 4 期，第 22 頁。
2　蔡定劍：《立法權與立法權限》，載《法學研究》1993 年第 5 期，第 4 頁。

立法權的實施仍然遵從使用權和所有權可以分離的原則。

（2）立法權的行使方式除了上述的可分離性外，還有體系性的特徵。作為一項國家權能，立法權區別於行政權和司法權，三者截然不同。但是，因為立法權的所有權和使用權可以分離，所以行政機關和司法機關亦存在行使立法權的機會，比如政府立法和判例立法，亦屬於立法權的一部分。早期的啟蒙思想家們認為，立法權只能由國家主權的代表機關行使，這一傳統理論至今仍得到許多國家的認可。現代國家事務複雜程度越來越高，立法機關應對的立法工作亦越來越繁重，立法工作全部由立法機關完成已不太可能，各國的行政機關，特別是地方政府亦需要進行大量的立法工作，但國家立法機關的性質和地位並沒有因此而改變。在許多國家的憲法和法理上，仍然堅持立法權是立法機關專有的權力，而不承認行政機關有立法權。例如，日本憲法第 41 條規定，國會是最高國家權力機關，是國家唯一的立法機關。美國憲法第 1 條規定，本憲法所授予的立法權，均屬於由參議院和眾議院所組成的合眾國國會。法國憲法第 34 條規定，所有法律均須議會通過。比利時憲法第 26 條規定，立法權由國王、眾議院和參議院共同行使。西班牙憲法第 26 條規定，總議會執行國家立法權。意大利憲法第 70 條規定，立法職能由兩院集體行使。[1] 上述國家的憲法條文都明確規定立法權屬於立法機關，但是現實中都存在政府立法的情況，即是立法機關通過委託授權的方式授權政府行使立法權，且這種授權立法受到立法機關的監督，立法機關有權收回委託授權。故此，不能認為政府機關擁有立法權，政府機關的立法是立法機關立法權的組成部分。

二、緊急立法權的權力譜系

（一）緊急立法權與國家權力的關係

國家權力可分為立法權、行政權和司法權，在緊急狀態下，三權演變為立法機關緊急權、行政機關緊急權和司法機關緊急權。為了更好地應對危機，國家緊急權力的行使需要三方聯動，涉及三權的配合。西方國家宣導的三權分立憲政原則在一定程度上要轉變成三權合作的模式，以便集中所有國家機關的力量來應對危機。[2] 下文將闡釋緊急狀態下國家權力，即立法權、行政權和司法權三權的嬗變。

1. 立法權主體的轉變

1　各國憲法的規定內容參見蔡定劍：《立法權與立法權限》，載《法學研究》1993 年第 5 期，第 3-4 頁。
2　郭春明：《緊急狀態法律制度研究》，北京：中國檢察出版社 2004 年版，第 105-119 頁。

立法機關是人民行使國家權力的重要組織，其形式表現為代議機關，其制度為議會制度，是民主鬥爭的過程中建立起來的民意代表機構。立法權以人民主權、社會契約、三權分立等原則和理論為基礎，以議會、國會、人民代表大會等為組織形式。正常時期國家立法權主要由立法機關行使，立法機關是立法權的絕對主體。只有當緊急狀態出現時，國家權力很大程度上集中由行政機關來實施，此時的立法權亦隨之轉移到行政機關，這時緊急立法權的主體就由行政機關擔任。然而，立法機關的監督職能並沒有因為緊急狀態的出現和立法權主體的轉變而喪失，仍然需要對緊急立法權的行使進行監督和制約，以保證國家緊急權力行使過程中的合憲性。

2. 行政權內容的擴張

隨著社會的發展，在國家追求和平、穩定、發展的環境下，各國行政機關承擔的公共事務管理工作越來越廣泛，管理的事務越來越複雜，於是行政立法活動亦越來越頻繁。儘管如此，並沒有因為行政立法活動的增加而破壞了立法機關立法的體系，正常狀態下立法權仍然屬於立法機關。但是，行政機關逐漸變成現代政治制度和國家治理的核心，國家權力的實施亦逐漸從傳統的"議會中心"向"行政中心"演變。這主要是由行政機關自身在公共事務管理方面的優勢決定的。行政機關承擔著國家治理的各個領域和具體工作，具有組織、人力、資源上的天然優勢，在正常狀態下的國家治理中措施更直接、效率更高。這種高效率的管理以及組織、人力、資源上的天然優勢讓行政機關在應對緊急情況時能夠快速有效作出反應。因此，國家緊急權力的行使必須以行政機關為中心，立法權和司法權向行政權集中，讓行政機關充分發揮自身優勢，集中整合各方力量應對緊急情況，這當中就包含行政機關行使立法機關的立法權，演變為行政機關的緊急立法權。雖然權力的集中使得行政機關在行使緊急權力時存在濫用的風險，因此要對其進行必要的監督，但是此種監督要保持謙抑。行政機關在應對緊急狀況時的主要地位和作用是國家生存必不可少的重要保障。

3. 司法權的削弱

司法權的實施有賴於當事人的告訴，司法機關不會主動、積極地去啟動司法程序，實行的是不告不理的消極原則，這一原則決定了司法機關在應對緊急狀態、恢復社會秩序時具有一定的消極性和滯後性。如果緊急情況可以通過司法程序來處理，那麼很大程度上就不能認為是緊急情況了，因為司法流程需要耗費一定的時間，而緊急情況需要即時處理。但是司法權在應對緊急情況時的消極性和滯後性並不等同於司法權在緊急狀態下的作用是可有可無的。司法權所提供的司法救濟在消弭緊急權行使對人權克減造成的負面影響以及恢復國家機關合法、權威形象方面具有不可取代的作用，是保障人權和法治的最後一道屏障。雖然司法權在應對緊急狀態時不可或缺，但是世界各國的國情各異，不同國家的憲法規定和實踐存在很大差異，主要表現在緊急狀態下普通司法權轉移到軍事機關或行政機關的範圍和程度，以及司法機關是否享有對行政機關緊急權包括緊急立法權等的實施進行司法審查的權力這兩個方面。

綜上所述，在緊急狀態下，立法權在國家權力體系中由立法機關轉移到了行政機關，演變成行政機關緊急立法權，主要是根據緊急狀態制定相應的法律或頒佈具有法律效力的命令。在正常狀態下的現代社會中，行政立法權已經成為行政機關行使行政管理職能的一種重要方式，這種方式彌補了立法機關進行立法時在程序、效率、數量等方面存在的不足，成為現代國家立法活動中的一個重要形式。在緊急狀態下，如果立法機關癱瘓，行政機關就通過立法或頒佈具有法律效力的緊急命令的形式行使緊急立法權，其可行性和必要性毋庸置疑。因此，許多國家的憲法都對行政機關行使緊急立法權予以肯定。

（二）緊急立法權與三權分立原則的關係

在緊急狀態中，三權分立的原則雖然在一定程度上轉變為三權合作，但是三權分立應有的監督之意並沒有喪失。緊急立法權的實施主要體現了三權的合作，同時，為了避免緊急立法權力被濫用，亦需要三權之間的互相監督，即對緊急立法權的立法監督、司法監督和行政監督。對緊急權的監督最重要的內容是對行政緊急權進行監督，而對行政緊急權進行監督又主要體現在對行政機關緊急立法權的監督。立法機關對緊急立法權的監督主要通過正常狀態下的立法來實現，是一種前置的監督。立法機關的監督還體現在對緊急狀態的決定和宣佈等，這是緊急立法權開啟的前提。對緊急立法權的行政監督主要體現為內部的協調和政治責任的追究，即對緊急立法制定程序的設置以及事後對緊急立法實施效果的評估。司法機關對緊急立法權的監督主要發生在緊急狀態結束之後，審查的依據主要是比例原則，可以對緊急立法進行合法性審查和合理性審查，確保行政機關与行政相對人在特殊狀態下保持權力与權利關係的協調。然而，相對於緊急狀態下立法權、司法權和行政權的三權監督問題，其協調合作問題更為重要。行政機關在緊急狀態下的作用要大於立法機關和司法機關，其中行政機關的緊急立法權是最重要的一種權力，突發事件的突然性、緊迫性、嚴重性決定了只有行政機關才能勝任緊急立法的職責。立法機關是通過合議的方式來表達國家意志，司法是事後的行為，與行政機關的應急措施相比總是太遲了。在世界上絕大多數國家的憲法和實踐中，對緊急狀態的決定或宣佈都由行政機關來實施，而且行政機關的這種行為被明確排除在司法審查之外，即使一些國家規定事後可以由立法機關予以追認或司法機關予以審查，亦都表現了對行政機關行使緊急立法權方面的尊重和克制態度。[1] 因此，這並不意味著三權分立原則不能對行政機關緊急立法權進行約束，而是說這種約束必須保持謙抑的態度。

（三）緊急立法權與一般立法權的關係

一般立法權和緊急立法權是同一立法權在不同情勢下的表現形式，其本質都是國家立法權，但它們在行使的主體、內容、權力來源、權力範圍以及立法程序等方面卻有很大的區別。一般立法權是在國家正常狀態下主要由立法機關行使，立法機關亦可以通過授權的方式將立法權委託行政機關行使，行政機關根據授權範圍和內容進行特定的立法活動，但並不因此獲得立法權，立法機關可以收回授

1　王旭坤：《緊急不避法治——政府如何應對突發事件》，北京：法律出版社2009 年版，第 92-94 頁。

權。緊急立法權則是一國在緊急狀態下為了應對一般立法權在效率和範圍上的不足，為了更及時高效地解決危機，而將原本屬於立法機關的立法權通過憲法授權的方式，集中到行政機關行使。為了避免行政機關立法權擴張和集中可能帶來的權力濫用，立法機關和司法機關承擔了對緊急立法權監督的職責。由此可見，緊急立法權的內容與一般立法權無異，但立法程序更加簡便，亦更容易被濫用。兩者都在憲政和法治的狀態下實施，緊急立法權必須由正常狀態下的憲法和法律提前作出具體規定和安排，且在緊急狀態消失後，緊急立法權應該回歸一般立法權。

三、緊急立法權的構成和特徵

（一）緊急立法權的構成

"權力必須配備若干要素才能構成完整的權力，它包括：權力主體，即國家權力的擁有者和實施者；權力對象，即國家權力實施的對象；權力目的，即國家權力實施所要達到的目標；權力手段，即實施國家權力的各種措施；權力結果，即實施國家權力的效益和後果。"[1] 完整的國家緊急權要具備的要素同樣應當是權力主體、對象、目

---

[1] 公丕祥主編：《法理學》，上海：復旦大學出版社 2002 年版，第 199-200 頁。

的、手段以及結果。[1] 下文我們將從實體要件和程序要件兩個層面對緊急立法權的構成進行闡述。

1. 實體要件

（1）緊急立法權的權力主體

從當今世界各國的憲法和法律規範來看，緊急立法權的主體構成形式大致可以分為以下三種：一是集體形式，即主要由立法機關、行政機關共用緊急立法權，強調權力的分享和平等；二是個體形式，即由行政機關或行政首領單獨承擔緊急立法權；三是集體與個體結合的形式，以一方為主，另一方為輔，強調權力的相互制約。三種主體形式相較而言各有優劣，集體形式的權力主體更加強調決策過程的民主性和制約性，個體形式則表現出權力主體決策的效率性、主動性和針對性等優勢，集體與個體結合的形式則主要出於對純粹個體決策中可能產生的權力濫用的顧忌，既強調個體決策的效率，又強調對個體決策必須施加監督。鑒於緊急事件會對國家的安全、利益甚至生存造成威脅和破壞，及時消除危機、恢復正常秩序應當成為國家的首要行動，這就決定了緊急立法權的主體首先要在最大程度上滿足迅速消除危機這一任務，那麼緊急立法權的主

---

[1] 王禎軍：《國家緊急權的理論與實踐》，北京：法律出版社 2015 年版，第 50-62 頁。

體就必須能夠充分滿足主動性、高效性和針對性的要求。同時，要求緊急立法權主體的設置能夠最大化地發揮國家緊急權的功能。亦就是說，緊急立法權主體本身應具有能夠實現多種權力集中的權威性，能夠最迅速、最有效地收集各種資訊和調集各種資源。在緊急狀態下，憲法列舉的正常狀態下的集體形式將癱瘓，因為這種互相制約的構造無法及時高效地應對危機，因此，許多國家的憲法明確將緊急權力授予個體形式的主體，即行政機關。

（2）緊急立法權的權力客體

緊急立法權的客體包括物、非物質財富、行為結果，但與正常狀態下的法律關係客體相比，由於緊急狀態的特殊性，緊急立法權客體呈現出一些自身的特點。緊急狀態通常是很難預見或無法預見的，往往很突然發生，有著很大的破壞性，需要及時應對才能降低損失。[1] 緊急立法權的行使是以緊急狀態為基礎和依據，故緊急立法權的客體跟緊急狀態關係密切，甚至有些客體在社會正常狀態下是不會出現的，比如政府在緊急狀態下做出的應急徵收徵用行為。另外，由於緊急狀態的存在，為了更好地應對危機，

---

1 Oren Gross and Fionnuala Ni Aoldin, *Law in Times of Crisis: Emergency Powers in Theory and Practice*, New York: Cambridge University Press, 2006, pp. 5-6.

緊急立法權對客體的限制會比正常狀態下有所擴張，主要表現在對正常狀態下公民權利的克減。但是這種克減不是絕對的，會受到國家憲法、甚至國際人權公約的制約。

（3）緊急立法權的權力結果

緊急立法權的結果是指權力主體通過簡化的立法程序，使相關應急法律快速通過和實施，進而化解危機並使得國家和社會恢復正常狀態的效益和後果。因為在應急處理的實踐中，權力主體所立之緊急法律通常會採取一些特殊的措施，使得正常狀態下的憲法秩序受到改變，所以通常會伴隨克減公民權利的產生。雖然這種克減權利的目的是希望能通過應急措施及時有效地消除危機，恢復社會的正常秩序，維護國家的生存，但其對憲法秩序和原則的挑戰，會受到非議、甚至反對。鑒於各國民主和法治狀態的不同，緊急立法權行使的結果亦不盡相同，大致可以分為以下三種情況：一是緊急立法得以通過，並順利實施且取得預期效果；二是緊急立法得以順利通過，但實施和取得的效果不理想；三是緊急立法通過受阻，無法實施。由此可見，緊急狀態的複雜性導致緊急立法權的權力結果具有不確定性。

2. 程序要件

緊急立法權之所以能實施，是因為它具有實施的具體程序，如果沒有這些具體程序，緊急立法權就無法實現預期的目的，最終使得權力落空。因此，程序是緊急立法權必不可少的構成要件。緊急立法權的程序可以分為廣義和狹義兩個方面：廣義的緊急立法權的程序包括緊急立法權的請求、決定、批准、宣佈、期限和延長；[1] 狹義的緊急立法權的程序包括權力主體實施緊急立法權時可以採取的各種立法措施，即相關緊急法律的制定權、提案權、再授權、公佈權和批准權。緊急立法權屬於行政緊急權的內容，廣義的緊急立法權程序很大程度上依託於行政緊急權程序。因為行政緊急權與立法緊急權、司法緊急權都屬於國家緊急權，所以三者的程序基本一致，廣義的緊急立法權程序依託於國家緊急權的程序。狹義的緊急立法權程序則區別於一般的立法權程序。因為緊急狀態的突發性和嚴重性，緊急立法權的實施必須及時有效，如果按照一般立法權的程序則需經過較長的時間，就勢必延誤緊急狀態的處置，使得緊急立法權變成擺設，所以緊急立法權相比一般立法權在程序上更為簡單、高效。因為緊急立法權主體有權通過立法或頒佈緊急命令的形式克減國家機構在正常狀態下應當承擔的憲法和法律義務，而這些憲法和法律義

1　郭春明：《緊急狀態法律制度研究》，北京：中國檢察出版社 2004 年版，第 66-83 頁。

務主要涉及對公民基本權利的保護，所以需要通過對制定的相關緊急法設置"先通過、後審議"以及"有效期限"的方式來對緊急立法權進行制約，這亦是緊急立法權與一般立法權最大的區別。

（二）緊急立法權的特徵

David Bonner 基於英美憲法和行政法的角度認為，國家緊急權力有三個主要特徵：一是有憲法上的依據，即憲法規定了其只能在國家宣佈進入緊急狀態之後才能夠行使；二是它是屬於行政機關的自由裁量權，不受憲法規範的約束；三是它是臨時性的，在緊急狀態結束之後就停止行使。[1] 內地學者郭春明認為國家緊急權具有以下特點：一是國家緊急權具有一定程度的超憲性；二是國家緊急權的行使目的是為了恢復正常的社會秩序；三是國家緊急權的行使具有不同於正常狀態下的國家權力的特點；四是國家緊急權的行使會對民主憲政產生一定的負面影響，國家在行使該項權力時必須慎重。[2] 另一位國內學者馬懷德認為國家緊急權具有以下特徵：一是屬於憲法的特徵，即憲政獨裁；二是權力集中與擴張的特徵；三是消極除礙的特徵；

1　參見徐高、莫紀宏：《外國緊急狀態法律制度》，北京：法律出版社 1994 年版，第 68 頁。

2　郭春明：《緊急狀態法律制度研究》，北京：中國檢察出版社 2004 年版，第 98-102 頁。

四是急迫性與短暫性的特徵。以上觀點雖然是針對國家緊急權，但由於緊急立法權屬於國家緊急權，下文將從以上國家緊急權的特徵來歸納總結出緊急立法權的三個特徵。

1. 緊急立法權的從屬性

隨著緊急立法在世界範圍內越來越受重視，各國基本都通過國家憲法規定國家緊急權的制度。由此可見，緊急立法權一般來源於憲法的授權且不得與憲法相抵觸，儘管緊急立法權可能會改變憲政秩序或克減公民權利，但這並不代表緊急立法權超越憲法。相反地，緊急立法權是為了恢復憲政秩序且是暫時性的，其最終目的還是為了維護憲法的實施，並沒有超越憲法的規定，而是從屬於憲法。

2. 緊急立法權的有限性

憲政國家的一切權力都是有限的，都受到憲法限制，憲法沒有賦予的權力，任何機關不得行使，[1] 緊急立法權亦不例外。緊急立法權具有集中性和擴張性，故更應該受到嚴格的限制。

（1）緊急立法權的內容有限。一方面，緊急立法的內容必須在憲法的授權範圍內；另一方面，超越憲法授權範圍的緊急立法行為屬於越權，越權無效。

1　鄧世豹：《授權立法的法理思考》，北京：中國人民公安大學出版社 2002 年版，第 54-56 頁。

（2）緊急立法權的權能有限。為了加強對緊急立法權的監督，依據緊急立法權制定的法律文件仍然必須經過監督機關的批准。只是不同於一般立法是批准後生效且長期有效，緊急立法可以先生效後批准，而且有一定的有效期限。

（3）緊急立法權的行使方式有限。一般由行政機關實施，且不能再次將緊急立法權授出。

（4）緊急立法權的行使條件有限。緊急立法權必須根據實際需要行使。如果緊急狀態沒有嚴重到必須啟動緊急權時，不得使用緊急立法權來管理國家和社會。

3. 緊急立法權的靈活性

授權立法的生命在於其靈活性，或者說授權立法的產生是為了維持分權原則、滿足不斷變化的社會對立法的需要，使立法滿足不斷變化的客觀條件。因此，必須及時制定或修改法律實施細則，或者以立法的方式對突發事件進行一般性調整，以克服成文憲法的高度穩定性帶來的消極影響，保證有關政府機構靈活處理社會問題。授權立法是在憲法高度穩定性、分權原則權威性與社會對政府職能靈活性的需要之間的一種平衡。

（1）緊急立法權的靈活性表現在立法形式的多樣性。行政機關除了可以根據緊急狀態制定原先由立法機關制定的法律外，不同層級的行政機關可以根據緊急狀態制定符合自己權力範圍的行政法律文件，如此，緊急立法權行使主體可以根據實際情況靈活選擇合適的立法形式。

（2）緊急立法權的靈活性體現在立法時機的把握。由於緊急狀態的複雜性和不確定性，何時進行緊急立法最有效？緊急立法的持續時間多長最能保障公民權利？緊急立法權行使主體可以根據緊急狀態的實際情況做出靈活的安排和取捨，從而有利於緊急立法權的效用合理化和最大化。

（3）緊急立法權的靈活性體現在立法程序的可變性。現代各國一般立法程序都有嚴格、明確的規定。但是為了提高緊急立法的效率，緊急立法的程序得到簡化，允許例外情況的出現，這使得緊急立法權的行使更加靈活高效。

第二節　緊急立法權的結構和功能

　　緊急立法權的權力結構包括縱向權力結構和橫向權力結構兩個方面。緊急立法權的功能包括維護國家生存的必要手段、恢復正常憲法秩序的法律保障等內容。

一、緊急立法權的結構

（一）緊急立法權的縱向權力結構

　　緊急狀態必然導致國家層面與地方層面在事權、人權和財權上的變化。正常狀態下，單一制國家或複合制國家的事權、人權和財權基本上都是體現國家層面對地方層面的集中控制，只是單一制國家集中控制的強度比複合制國家更大。緊急狀態發生以後，為了讓地方政府在應對危機時更加及時、準確和有效，應在確保主權統一的基礎上，對原有的國家權力分配制度進行調整，國家層面應該給予地方層面在處理緊急狀態上相匹配的人、財、物權配比，逐步給地方政府更大的議價能力，提高其博弈能力，適當擴大地方政府的自治權力，尤其是緊急狀態中的應急處置權力。而國家權力分配的落實很大程度要依靠立法，故賦予行政機關緊急立法權，特別是地方政府的緊急立法權，能夠切實提高地方政府的應急處置能力。

然而，世界上無論是採用單一制還是複合制的國家，其國家權力分配都是一個重要且複雜的問題，主要涉及國家層面與地方層面在事權、人權和財權上如何分配，該問題在正常狀態下就是個難題，在緊急狀態下更是如此。筆者贊成沈歸教授的觀點，[1]認為中央和地方在緊急立法權的縱向權力結構設置上可作如下設計：一是緊急立法權縱向權力結構整體劃分為國家層面的保留和地方層面的保留；二是緊急立法權縱向權力結構的具體實施可以分為：排除妨礙、請求說明、緊急創制、特別程序。其中，中央保留是指凡全國性或者涉及省際關係的緊急或者救援措施，或者在大、中城市的重大緊急或者救援措施，當由中央進行決策（當然，在全國人大及其常委會和國務院及其部門之間，仍然需要一定的權力劃分）。地方保留是指除上述措施以外的緊急或救援措施，若非限制人身自由的緊急措施（現行《立法法》要求必須由全國人大或其常委會制定的法律才能規定），授權省級人大及其常委會以地方性法規或決議、省級政府以地方政府規章或決定規定之。在中央

---

1 沈歸：《"SARS" 拷問之下的 " 各自為政 "》，載《21 世紀經濟報導》2003 年 5 月 13 日。

或者省級地方規定的措施以外的緊急或救援措施，省級以下地方確實需要實施的，當報經省級地方批准，並報中央備案。排除妨礙是指凡地方出現任何妨礙緊急或者救援措施順利實施的情形，中央和省級地方都有權作出決策或者採取必要的、適當的措施予以排除。請求說明是指省級地方確實需要資金、設備、醫藥、人員等方面援助的，有權向中央提出請求。省級以下地方確實需要的，亦有權向省級地方請求幫助。緊急創制是指授權省級人大及其常委會和省級政府，在出現明確無誤的緊急狀態下，以地方性法規或決議、地方政府規章或決定的方式，規定與現有法律或國務院行政法規相抵觸的非常緊急措施。省級以下地方確實需要實施與法律或國務院行政法規相抵觸的非常緊急措施時，應當請求省級地方作出規定。特別程序是指省級地方在規定了與法律或國務院行政法規相抵觸的非常緊急措施以後，應當在一定期限內，向全國人民代表大會常務委員會或國務院請求確認有效。

（二）緊急立法權的橫向權力結構

國家的緊急權可以分為立法機關的緊急權、行政機關的緊急權和司法機關的緊急權，甚至還包括軍事機關的緊急權。[1] 然而，在國家緊急權的諸多內容中，為何只有行政機關的緊急權、特別是行政機關的緊急立法權最為突出和最受重視呢？這主要取決於緊急立法權橫向權力結構的集中性和擴張性。緊急狀態下行政權力的橫向集中和擴展是有歷史實例和經驗的，各國通過憲法和法律對這種橫向的集中和擴張進行規範和制約，體現了緊急立法權橫向權力結構的合法性。

　　緊急立法權的設置主要目的是為了及時、有效地應對緊急狀態，其橫向權力結構設置可作如下設計：一是集體形式與個體形式結合的主體模式。緊急狀態下，憲法列舉的各項國家權力主體分立或互相控制將不可避免地癱瘓，因為這種機械的構造無法及時高效地應對危機，緊急立法權等國家緊急權必須集中到合適的單個主體來實施。正因為如此，許多國家的憲法明確將緊急權力授予個體化的行政主體，不同於正常狀態下強調程序和民主的集體化國家權力橫向結構設置。當然，強調程序和民主的集體化國家權力橫向結構的主體設置亦可以應用於緊急狀態，只是在效率和效果上比個體化的主體設置差，但亦並非一無是處。考慮到緊急立法權具有增設憲法義務的權能，特別是

1　戚建剛：《法治國家架構下的行政緊急權力》，北京：北京大學出版社 2008 年版，第 15 頁。

具有克減公民基本權利的權能，會對公民的基本權利造成極大的影響，故此，在緊急立法權主體的設定上亦要考慮到對立法主體的制約，防止權力的濫用。而集體化主體所表現出的監督功能正好契合對緊急立法權主體設置的這一制度化的要求。因此，為了在迅速消除危機與保護人權兩者間作出平衡，集體形式與個體形式結合的模式相對比較科學，既能有效保證行政機關緊急立法權最大程度的實施和發揮作用，又能將立法機關和司法機關作為行政機關緊急立法權的監督主體，確保緊急立法權不被濫用。二是行政機關緊急立法權的運作機制。緊急狀態的特點在於其發生和發展過程具有突然性、緊迫性和嚴重性，這就需要行政機關在有限的時間和條件下果斷、迅速地採取緊急措施，主動和積極應對危機，同時還需要協調不同的國家機關，從而優化資源，發揮國家機關整體功效。緊急狀態的特點和應急要求決定了只有行政機關才能勝任緊急狀態下的立法權職責。

二、緊急立法權的功能

在社會正常狀態下，國家依靠憲法可以建立起良好的憲法秩序，據此維護國家的安全和生存。然而一旦出現緊急狀態，正常狀態下的憲法秩序通常受到破壞。因此，當國家在面臨緊急狀態的時候如何克服危機、恢復秩序是一個關係國家生存的問題，此時的緊急立法權是政府部門應對緊急狀態的利器，有著十分重要的價值功能：一是緊急狀態時期維護國家生存的必要手段，二是恢復正常憲法秩序的法律保障。[1] 除此之外，緊急立法權還有以下功能。

（一）完善國家緊急管理法律制度

隨著各國對緊急狀態處理的重視，越來越多的法律制度被逐步建立，但是由於法律制度的滯後性，以及緊急狀態的複雜性、不確定性，經常導致下面兩種被動的情況：一是因緊急狀態法律制度的龐雜，在理解和適用方面出現很大的差異，這會引起民眾對相關法律制度的質疑，不利於緊急狀態的處理；二是法律制度的缺失，可能是已有法律制度的不完善導致應急處理時某一方面沒有依據，亦可能是某一方面法律制度的缺失導致無法應對當下的緊急狀態。為了解決上述問題，必須充分發揮和利用緊急立法權的功能，適時制定出臺具有針對性的相關法律制度，完善緊急狀態的法律制度。

（二）保障公民的基本權利

在應對緊急狀態時，經常由於緊急狀態的急迫性和嚴

1　王禎軍：《國家緊急權的理論與實踐》，北京：法律出版社 2015 年版，第 64-65 頁。

重性，需要採取一些有別於正常狀態下的特殊措施，導致對公民的基本權利造成克減。為了使克減有法可依，並對行政緊急權的集中和擴張進行制約，以保障公民的基本權利，需要對一些臨時採取的措施進行緊急立法，以法律手段保護公民的知情權和獲得司法救濟的權利。

（三）規範緊急權力的行使

緊急權力的行使可能會對公民權利造成消極影響，要將消極影響降到最低，最終還是要依靠對緊急權力行使的規範。由於緊急狀態的變數很大，應急措施亦需要經常修改調整或重新制定，這就需要緊急立法權來填補緊急狀態下一般立法權缺位的漏洞，從實體和程序上對緊急權力的行使進行規範，以求上述功能的全部實現。

第三節　緊急立法權的法理證成

　　緊急立法權應具有合理性、合法性和正當性。關於緊急立法權的合理性，我們同樣亦從感性和理性兩個方面來分析。緊急立法權的合法性體現為具有現實的法律依據，並受到監督制約。緊急立法權的正當性要求緊急立法權的實施必須符合該國的憲法規定。

一、合理性

　　何謂合理性？主要指合乎規律。以下我們從感性和理性兩個方面來分析。從感性方面去看待緊急立法權時，我們經常只看到了緊急立法權的一些表象特徵，比如緊急立法權對憲政秩序的破壞以及對公民權利的克減。另外，雖然很多國家的憲法文本都規定了緊急狀態條款，但由於條款內容簡單抽象，緊急立法權的啟動和制定程序都受人質疑，這些都是其消極和負面的部分，如果我們只看到這些表象就容易感性地認為緊急立法權不合理。理性和感性不能截然分開，我們要在感性的基礎上，通過科學、客觀、全面的思維分析，認識到緊急立法權制定的相關緊急法雖然在一定程度上破壞了原先的憲政秩序，亦對公民基本權利造成一些消極影響，然而，這些不是緊急立法權的終極功能和目的，其本質上還是希望通過採取緊急立法，最終達到恢復憲政秩序，保障國家生存和公民權利的目的，而且有一定期限的限制。雖然其啟動和制定過程容易受人質疑，但是還是會在憲法規定的框架內合法、公開、有序地進行。

綜上所述，緊急立法權的實施符合緊急狀態的應對規律，是通過權力暫時性的集中和擴張，達到恢復社會秩序的目的，故緊急立法權具備合理性。

二、合法性

從各國憲法上的相關規定來看，緊急立法權的合法性可以從以下幾個方面來分析。

（一）緊急立法權的法律依據

制定法律原本是立法機關的主要職能，當遇到緊急狀態時，由於國家權力向行政機關集中，加上立法機關的工作效率相對低下，甚至可能因緊急狀態出現癱瘓的情況，顯然立法機關無法滿足緊急立法權的高效性和急迫性要求。因此，緊急狀態下立法機關的立法主要是通過憲法授權的方式由行政機關行使，即通過憲法授權將緊急立法權授予行政機關行使，所以憲法是緊急立法權的法律依據。除此之外，行政機關還擁有緊急狀態下的職權立法授權，行政機關的職能一般是由憲法或組織法等法律文件規定的，這些法律文件在緊急狀態下仍然存在，是緊急立法權的法律依據。

（二）緊急立法權的法律約束

雖然行政機關的緊急立法權來自憲法的授權，該項權力原本屬於立法機關，但這並不意味著立法機關因此喪失了對立法的監督權。因為立法機關作為民意代表機關，對涉及行使國家權力和限制人民權利的重要事項行使最終的決定權。在緊急狀態下，行政權力的集中和擴張，使得國家立法機關對行政緊急權行使的監督顯得更為重要。很多國家的憲法都作了具體的規定，主要表現為以下幾個方面：一是批准進入緊急狀態的決定；二是決定緊急狀態的期限及緊急狀態的延長申請；三是對行政機關在緊急狀態期間所制定的緊急法予以批准；四是撤銷行政機關在緊急狀態下所制定的不適當的緊急法。

另外，因為緊急狀態下應急措施的採取、公民權利的克減等容易造成對憲政秩序和公民權利的損害，當出現損害結果時，必須為當事人提供維權的途徑。相較於立法機關宏觀的、事前的監督，司法機關的監督屬於具體的、事後的監督，從更好地保障公民個體權利的角度來看，司法監督更具有現實作用和意義。

綜上所述，緊急立法權可以找到現實的法律依據，亦受到立法機關和司法機關的監督制約，這確保其具有合法性。

三、正當性

根據《辭海》的解釋，正當性是指在倫理學上符合道德原則和規範的行為，亦指社會對這一行為的肯定評價。[1] 在法治國家中，所有國家機關活動的基礎和依據都是由憲法規範確認的。確定政權構成、賦予國家機關權力、調整不同國家機關之間的關係是憲法的重要功能。在正常狀態下，國家的立法機關、行政機關和司法機關各自行使憲法賦予的職權，無論是立法權、行政權和司法權之間，還是行政權與公民的基本權利之間，均處在一種相互制約又相互平衡的關係狀態。然而，在緊急狀態下，由於行政緊急權具有對正常狀態下憲法權力與憲法權利的否定作用，行政機關採取包括克減公民基本權利在內的緊急措施以應對危機的過程，實質上是打破國家機關之間、行政權

---

1 《辭海》(1999 年版縮印本) (音序)，上海：上海辭書出版社 2002 年版，第 2174 頁。

與公民基本權利之間的平衡，並重新建立新的平衡的過程。由於這一過程有可能違背"限制公權力，保護基本權利"的法治理念，會對正常狀態下的憲法秩序產生影響，所以必須由憲法加以調整和規範。[1]

另外，作為政治法的憲法，其具體內容反映了一種政治選擇。在一個特定的國家裏，憲法條文的內容與所調整的憲法關係往往體現該國的理念與政策。根據統治行為理論，宣佈緊急狀態被作為免受司法審查的政治行為之一。然而，在許多國家的緊急狀態實踐中，緊急立法權的行使會超出"維護國家生存"的底線，經常被用來作為減損人權的手段。如學者所言，"現代法治不允許法律不加限制地交給政府一張空白支票，讓政府在緊急狀態下任意確定自己行使何種權力"[2]，因此，在現代法治國家中，宣佈緊急狀態必須具有憲法規範的依據，並接受憲法的監督。就如聯合國人權事務委員會強調的，在宣佈國家進入緊急狀態並可能引起克減公民權利時，國家採取的應急行動必須符合其憲法的規定。[3]

1　王禎軍：《論行政緊急權的憲法規制》，載《河北法學》2017 年第 7 期，第 52-53 頁。

2　姜明安：《突發事件下行政權力的規範》，載《法制日報》2003 年 5 月 15 日。

3　Human Rights Committee, Comment No. 29: *States of Emergency* (Article 4), CCPR/C/21/Rev.1/Add.11, para. 2, paras. 5-6.

綜上所述，由於法律是道德的最低底線，緊急立法權的實施必須符合一國的憲法規定，最終使得行政機關的緊急立法權具備正當性。

第二章

香港特區行政長官緊急立法權的學理分析

香港特區行政長官緊急立法權的憲制依據是《緊急條例》。該條例由港英立法局在 1922 年通過，規定總督會同行政局有權在“緊急情況”或“公共危險”情況下直接通過總督認為適當的規例。當香港於 1997 年回歸中國時，《緊急條例》與許多其他原有法律一樣，成為香港特別行政區法律制度的一個組成部分。香港特區行政長官緊急立法權所指的“緊急”是指《緊急條例》規定的“緊急情況”和“危害公安”，有別於《中華人民共和國憲法》（以下簡稱《中國憲法》）和《香港基本法》規定的“緊急狀態”。行政長官的緊急立法亦稱附屬立法、附屬法例或附屬法規，但這種附屬立法與一般附屬立法存在重大區別，行政長官立法的自主性很高。借鑒澳門《關於訂定內部規範的法律制度》中的"獨立行政法規"概念[1]，可稱這種緊急附屬立法為"獨立附屬立法"或"獨立附屬法規"。香港特區行政長官緊急立法權的功能，除了具有緊急立法的一般功能，還具有特別功能。

---

1 《關於訂定內部規範的法律制度》俗稱"澳門立法法"，把行政長官制定的行政法規分為獨立行政法規和補充性行政法規。前者是行政長官依據《澳門基本法》制定，是就法律沒有規範的事宜設定初始性的規範；後者是行政長官依據立法會立法制定，為執行法律而訂定所必需的具體措施。

第一節　香港特區緊急立法權的沿革

緊急立法權在香港經歷了港督的緊急立法權到行政長官會同行政會議緊急立法權的演變過程。港督的緊急立法權最初來自《皇室訓令》，香港《戒嚴法》亦賦予港督緊急立法權。而行政長官會同行政會議的緊急立法權可以溯源到香港《戒嚴法》。

一、港督的緊急立法權

港督的緊急立法權，最初來自《皇室訓令》。依此憲制性法律文件，港督擁有緊急立法權，即遇到緊急情況，議案可以在一次立法會議之內通過"三讀"的程序，立即由港督簽署並生效。最有名的例子是 1974 年香港一些警務人員不滿廉政公署調查他們貪污受賄的犯罪行為，不僅進行了遊行示威，還威脅要抵抗法律的執行，想要迫使廉政公署撤銷對他們的調查和起訴，由此香港的法治秩序、社會治安和政治穩定遭到嚴重威脅。時任香港港督麥理浩立即召開臨時立法局會議，在短短三十分鐘內就"三讀"通過了一項專門的緊急立法，授權警務處處長第一時間開除不服從法律的警務人員，並利用輿論宣傳讓大家檢舉那些違法的警務人員的行為，於是危機得以解除。[1]可見，回歸前的香港緊急立法權是存在的，且是由港督享有並掌控。

現今香港的《緊急條例》可以溯源到 1844 年由港英立法機關通過後又被英國政府廢除的《戒嚴法》。《緊急條例》訂立以來，港英政府或用其來應對大型的社會運動，例如 1925 年的省港大罷工、1931 年的"灣仔反日騷動"、1956 年的"雙十暴動"和 1967 年的"六七風暴"等；或用其來應對其他緊急情況，如 1929 年的旱災、1932 年的霍亂、1950 年的硬幣短缺和 1973 年的石油危機等。2019 年，香港特區政府首次使用《緊急條例》訂立《禁止蒙面規例》，引起公眾對其合"憲"性的關注。

從香港《緊急條例》的演變歷史來看，英國曾經廢除了香港的《戒嚴法》，歷史上並沒有給過香港類似對威爾士、蘇格蘭的涉及"主權"和國家安全的緊急許可權。香港《緊急條例》與英國在本土制定的緊急法有本質的區別，其實質是英國或香港處理該地區社會緊急情況的法律依據，而不涉及國家"主權"與安全等問題，這點可以從

1　楊奇主編：《香港概論》（下），北京：中國社會科學出版社 1996 年版，第 30 頁。

歷史上香港援引《緊急條例》應對的緊急情況都是社會動亂或自然災害等得到印證。

二、行政長官會同行政會議的緊急立法權

1922 年港英立法局通過的《緊急條例》規定，總督會同行政局有權在"緊急情況"或"公共危險"下直接通過總督認為適當的規例。《緊急條例》的制定是為了應對 1922 年的香港海員罷工。1967 年，為了呼應中國內地的"文化大革命"，香港的一些左派人士在"反英、反暴力"的號召下，發起了"六七風暴"[1]。對此，港英政府進一步擴大賦予總督權力的範圍，授予總督直接處理通訊、出版、入境、逮捕、拘留和驅逐罷工工人等權力。

當香港於 1997 年回歸中國時，《緊急條例》與許多其他原有法律一樣，成為香港特別行政區法律制度的一個組成部分。《香港基本法》第 8 條亦規定，普通法、衡平法、條例、附屬立法及習慣法，除同本法相抵觸或經香港特別行政區的立法機關作出修改者外，均予以保留。1997

---

1 "六七風暴"，於 1967 年 5 月 6 日發動，同年 12 月份基本結束，是一場在"文化大革命"的影響下，香港左派人士展開的對抗港英政府的運動。由最初的罷工、示威，發展至後來的暗殺、炸彈放置和槍戰。風暴期間，至少造成包括 10 名警員在內的 51 人死亡，包括 212 名警員在內的 802 人受傷，1,936 人被檢控。

年 2 月，第八屆全國人民代表大會常務委員會第二十四次會議審議了香港特別行政區籌備委員會關於處理香港原有法律的建議，以及全國人民代表大會常務委員會根據《香港基本法》第 160 條作出的關於處理香港原有法律的決定。在本決定中，香港原有法律分為三種情況需要處理，而《緊急條例》屬於第三類，經修改後已成為香港特別行政區的法律。該條例中的"總督"修改為"行政長官"，內容幾乎保持不變。該條例保留的目的在於授予行政長官會同行政會議在香港出現"緊急情況"或"危害公安"時，可以及時訂立規例予以處理的權力。該條例第 2 條規定了訂立規例的權力：（1）香港特區行政長官會同行政會議在認為正在發生的事件屬於"緊急情況"或"危害公安"時，可訂立任何他們認為與公眾利益相符的規例。（2）在不損害第 1 款的一般性的原則下，行政長官會同行政會議訂立的規例涉及限制人身自由等十多種情形。（3）任何規例或依據該規例訂立的命令或規則，即使與任何成文法則中所載者有抵觸，仍具效力；而任何成文法則中任何條文如與任何規例或任何上述命令或規則有抵觸，則不論該條文是否在其實施過程中已根據第 2 款予以修訂、暫停或修改，只要上述規例、命令或規則仍屬有效，上述有抵觸之處並無效力。[1]條例第 3 條規定了罰則：（1）在不損害第 2 條所授予的權力的原則下，根據本條例訂立的規例可就任何罪行（不論該罪行屬違反該等規例的罪行或屬任何適用於香港的法律所訂的罪行），規定以任何刑罰及制裁（包括強制性終身監禁的最高刑罰，但不包括死刑）作為該罪行的懲罰，並可載有關於沒收、處置與保留在任何方面與上述罪行有關的物品的條文，以及關於撤銷或取消根據該等規例或其他任何成文法則發出的許可證、牌照、通行證或許可權文件的條文，而該等刑罰、制裁及條文是行政長官會同行政會議覺得為確保任何規例或法律的強制執行而屬必需或合宜的，或在其他方面符合公眾利益的。[2]（2）任何人如違反任何根據本條例訂立的規例，而該等規例並無規定其他刑罰或懲罰，則一經循簡易程序定罪，可處第 2 級罰款及監禁 2 年。[3]由此可見，《緊急條例》賦予香港特區行政長官緊急立法權的範圍很大，威懾力亦很強。

在此需要特別闡明的是《香港基本法》第 56 條有關規定與《緊急條例》第 2 條的關係。《香港基本法》第 56 條第 2 款規定，行政長官在作出重要決策、向立法會提交

---

1 《緊急情況規例條例》，由 1999 年第 71 號第 2 條修訂。
2 《緊急情況規例條例》，由 1993 年第 24 號第 24 條修訂；由 1999 年第 71 號第 3 條修訂。
3 《緊急情況規例條例》，2021 年第 5 號編輯修訂記錄。

法案、制定附屬法規和解散立法會前，須徵詢行政會議的意見，但人事任免、紀律制裁和緊急情況下採取的措施除外。該條款所規定的行政長官在緊急情況下採用的措施，應不包括根據《緊急條例》訂定附屬立法，因為《緊急條例》要求行政長官會同行政會議才可以訂定應對"緊急情況"或"危害公安"的附屬法規，這裏的"行政長官會同行政會議"（Chief Executive in Council）就是指在徵詢行政會議的意見後行事的行政長官[1]。否則，《緊急條例》就違反了《香港基本法》第 56 條第 2 款的規定。

---

1 《釋義及通則條例》第 3 條。

第二節　香港特區行政長官緊急立法權概要

香港特區行政長官緊急立法權所指的"緊急"是指《緊急條例》規定的"緊急情況"和"危害公安"，有別於《中國憲法》和《香港基本法》規定的"緊急狀態"。行政長官依照《緊急條例》的立法是附屬立法，但這種附屬立法與一般附屬立法存在重大區別。香港特區行政長官緊急立法的功能，除了具有前文所述的緊急立法的一般功能，還具有填補法制漏洞、豐富應急措施和拓展彈性空間等特別功能。

一、"緊急"內涵的釐清

由前文內容可見，在世界各國立法中，對緊急狀態的理解存在明顯區別。中國內地有學者認為，可以從廣義的角度理解緊急狀態，只要是擾亂社會正常秩序的事情都可稱之為緊急狀態。緊急狀態分輕重等級，將諸如普通刑事犯罪行為的威脅列為緊急狀態的屬於輕等級；將內戰、對外抵抗入侵等列為緊急狀態的屬於重等級。另外，還可以從狹義的角度理解緊急狀態，把緊急狀態理解成為發生在全國或其局部的、可以通過國家行政權就可以處理的危險事態。在採用狹義概念的這些國家中，戰爭通常被認為是一種獨立的狀態，戰爭與緊急狀態的性質不同，其處置的措施和手段亦不同。[1]

目前，對於香港特別行政區而言，《中國憲法》和《香港基本法》中的有關規定，以及香港特區《緊急條例》共同構成了涉及香港的緊急狀態法體系。時任香港特區行政長官林鄭月娥援引《緊急條例》制定《禁止蒙面規例》，是因為她認為香港出現了"危害公安"的情況，並沒有提及"緊急情況"，她還特意強調援引《緊急條例》制定《禁止蒙面規例》並不意味著香港進入了"緊急狀態"。另外，"緊急情況"與"緊急狀態"具有不同內涵，對這兩個詞語的闡釋是理解行政長官緊急立法權的關鍵。

（一）相關法條規定的"緊急"內容分析

1.《中國憲法》規定的緊急狀態

《中國憲法》第 67 條第 21 項規定，全國人民代表大會常務委員會行使下列職權：決定全國或者個別省、自治區、直轄市進入緊急狀態。《中國憲法》第 80 條規定，中華人民共和國主席根據全國人民代表大會的決定和全國人

1　徐高、莫紀宏：《外國緊急狀態法律制度》，北京：法律出版社 1994 年版，第 1-2 頁。

民代表大會常務委員會的決定，宣佈進入緊急狀態，宣佈戰爭狀態，發佈動員令。《中國憲法》第 89 條第 16 項規定，國務院行使下列職權：依照法律規定決定省、自治區、直轄市的範圍內部分地區進入緊急狀態。其中涉及到"緊急狀態"的概念，儘管《中國憲法》沒有對"緊急狀態"的文義進行解釋，但仍可以理解為國家層面的緊急權。根據《中國憲法》的根本法地位，其規定的"緊急狀態"必然是其他法律界定"緊急狀態"定義的依據。

2.《香港基本法》規定的緊急狀態

《香港基本法》是依據《中國憲法》制定的，對"緊急狀態"的文義解釋應該與《中國憲法》保持一致。《香港基本法》第 18 條規定，全國人民代表大會常務委員會決定宣佈戰爭狀態或因香港特別行政區內發生香港特區政府不能控制的危及國家統一或安全的動亂而決定香港特別行政區進入緊急狀態，中央人民政府可發佈命令將有關全國性法律在香港特別行政區實施。該條規定了香港"緊急狀態"的啟動條件，列明"因香港特別行政區內發生香港特區政府不能控制的危及國家統一或安全的動亂而決定香港特別行政區進入緊急狀態"，這與《中國憲法》規定的"緊急狀態"有所區別，是基於"一國兩制"以及中央與香港特別行政區之間關係作出的特別補充，可以理解為地方層面的緊急權。

3.《緊急條例》規定的緊急狀態

《緊急條例》第 2 條第 1 款規定，在香港特區行政長官會同行政會議認為發生的事件屬"緊急情況"或"危害公安"時，行政長官會同行政會議可以訂立他 / 她認為與公眾利益相符合的規例。行政長官會同行政會議啟動緊急權的條件是出現"緊急情況"或"危害公安"的情況，此種情況是否屬於《中國憲法》和《香港基本法》規定的"緊急狀態"的類型？《中國憲法》規定，全國人大常委會決定省、自治區、直轄市進入緊急狀態；國務院則決定省、自治區、直轄市的範圍內部分地區進入緊急狀態；而全國、省、自治區、直轄市是否進入緊急狀態只能由國家主席來宣佈。《香港基本法》第 18 條第 4 款規定，由全國人民代表大會常務委員會決定香港特區是否進入緊急狀態。回顧修例風波的整個過程，國家層面並沒有決定香港進入緊急狀態，行政長官亦並不是因應《香港基本法》第 18 條第 4 款規定而援引《緊急條例》，但是行政長官確實啟動了緊急立法權，其理由是"危害公安"，可見《緊急條例》規定的"緊急情況"和"危害公安"並非《中國憲法》和《香港基本法》規定的"緊急狀態"。

（二）香港特區行政長官緊急立法權中的"緊急"

1. "緊急情況"和"緊急狀態"的關係

《香港基本法》同時使用了"緊急情況"和"緊急狀態"，這兩者有什麼區別和聯繫呢？內地學者底高揚認為，這既是立法修辭技術的需要，也因為這兩個概念規定了不同的法律內容。緊急情況是一種事實狀態，而緊急狀態則是一種法律狀態，前者屬於描述性概念，後者屬於規範性概念。事實狀態是一種自然的、客觀的現實存在，是自然界或人類社會自發運動的結果，經常表現為自然災害、社會動亂、流行疾病等。而法律狀態則是國家機關依據事實和法定程序作出的法律擬制狀態，是法律主體理性決策或創設的一種具有法律效力的狀態，即緊急狀態是國家機關為了應對緊急情況而依據法定程序作出的具有法律效力的決定。[1]由此可見，"緊急情況"和"緊急狀態"是不同性質和內容的概念，"緊急狀態"出現必然存在"緊急情況"，但"緊急情況"卻不一定引起"緊急狀態"。

2. 行政長官實施緊急立法權的前提

行政長官實施緊急立法權的前提是"緊急情況"還是"緊急狀態"呢？《香港基本法》和《緊急條例》對此問題

1　底高揚：《論香港特別行政區行政長官的緊急立法權》，載《港澳研究》2021 年第 2 期，第 26 頁。

是有明確界定的。"緊急狀態"出現在《香港基本法》第18條第4款，即全國人民代表大會常務委員會決定宣佈戰爭狀態或因香港內部發生特別行政區政府不能控制的危及國家統一或安全的動亂，需要決定香港特別行政區進入緊急狀態時，中央政府可發佈命令將有關的全國性法律在香港實施。但《香港基本法》並未賦予行政長官緊急立法權，行政長官實施緊急立法權的法律依據是香港《緊急條例》。這就表明香港特區行政長官必須在發生"緊急情況"或"危害公安"時，才有權決定會同行政會議行使緊急立法權。

3. 發生"緊急情況"的判斷標準

何為"緊急情況"呢？其判斷標準可以從發生的時間、損害的程度、持續的時長、波及的範圍、引起的原因、損害的對象等方面進行考量，一般需要綜合多個因素才能做出判斷。有學者認為，"緊急情況"的判斷標準有其共同的規律，一般表現為嚴重性、急迫性、特殊性等方面，有的緊急情況發生前會出現一些苗頭或者徵兆，而有的緊急情況則是短時間內突然出現。緊急情況與正常情況的分界點往往不是某一個具體的時刻，而是一個動態的、持續發展演變的過程，緊急情況發生與否的判斷標準的核心在於衡量香港的整體安全和利益是否已經處於嚴重而緊迫的危險之中。這種危害難以制定量化標準，只能依賴於香港特區政府善意且理性的判斷。[1] 由此可見，"緊急情況"的判斷標準帶有強烈的主觀意識，難以由統一明確的標準判定，這亦造成了認定的困難，影響了"緊急情況"的宣告。

綜上所述，香港特區行政長官緊急立法權所指的"緊急"首先是指《緊急條例》規定的"緊急情況"，有別於《中國憲法》和《香港基本法》規定的"緊急狀態"。兩者的性質、內容不同，對國家和地方在緊急權的啟動和行使主體方面作了區分，避免了權力行使的混亂，亦使得香港特區行政長官在行使緊急立法權上有了正當的理由和依據。當然，"危害公安"亦是行政長官會同行政會議行使緊急立法權的理由和依據，《緊急條例》中沒有對"危害公安"進行解釋，其內涵可參考香港《公安條例》。

二、緊急立法的自主性

香港回歸前的附屬立法是由港英時代的立法局授權行政局、市政局等其他機構或政府官員為更好地實施條例而制定的，一般都是與條例相適應的配套規定或實施細則，

---

1 底高揚：《論香港特別行政區行政長官的緊急立法權》，載《港澳研究》2021 年第 2 期，第 26-27 頁。

其條文形式多表現為規則、規例和附例。對於香港附屬立法的性質，中國內地有學者認為，附屬立法是對條例實施的一種補充，內容涉及範圍很廣，包括公用事業和公益事業，如由市政局制定的有關娛樂業的規則，如由輪渡、電車公司制定且經總督會同行政局批准的通行規則，如以香港首席法官為首的規則委員會制定的香港最高法院案件處理規則等。附屬立法在一定程度上受到法院制約，香港特別行政區法院有權以越權或抵觸現行法、條文內容不合理、立法程序錯誤、立法權的轉讓委託無效等理由宣佈政府的附屬立法無效。[1] 可見，傳統意義上的香港附屬立法雖然內容涉及面廣，但只能是對條例實施進行細化，在某種程度上只具有附屬性，不具有自主性。

香港回歸後，保留下來的附屬立法成為香港法律體制的一大特色。但是在《香港基本法》規定的香港權力組織架構中，立法權屬於立法會，立法會制定的條例是進行附屬立法的前提條件，即條例是附屬立法權的源頭，因此，政府部門的附屬立法權亦應由條例規定。香港條例授予政府的附屬立法權必須嚴格依照條例的明確授權範圍和內容行使，這種授權授予的不是一般性的立法權，而是受到限

---

1 羅昶、喬克裕、高其才：《論香港法的淵源》，載《法學評論》1997 年第 4 期，第 22 頁。

制的立法權。同時，由於香港特別行政區的立法權只屬於立法會，政府亦不能依據自身職能進行獨立的行政立法。授權條例其實已經對政府的附屬立法權的形式和內容做了非常謹慎和明晰的規定，通常都會在條例中詳盡列舉出附屬立法的具體事項和內容，附屬立法通常不得超出條例授予的許可權的範圍。由於香港條例本身的內容一般都比較具體、詳盡，包括對實施條例的政府部門的職能、許可權、責任、行使權力的必要條件和程序，還有相對人尋求法律救濟的方式和途徑等，均有明晰的規定，因而，政府的附屬立法一般只需要依照條例有關授權的條文內容制定實施細則，最後的結果一般會比條例的內容更為詳細、瑣碎，篇幅一般較長。[1] 總之，對行政長官來說，制定附屬立法的自主性一般很低，不能 "越雷池半步"。

行政長官依照《緊急條例》的立法也是附屬立法，但這種附屬立法與一般附屬立法存在重大區別。如前所述，條例授權一般都詳盡列舉附屬立法的具體事項和範圍，但《緊急條例》給行政長官的授權只是概括性授權，並沒有詳盡列舉附屬立法的具體事項和範圍，這導致行政長官的緊急立法權受到限制的程度很小，自主性很高，行政長官

---

1 蕭金明：《香港行政法制的啟示 ——香港法治行政的觀察和聯想》，載《山東大學學報》2001 年第 1 期，第 3-4 頁。

依據《緊急條例》制定的緊急法亦不是對《緊急條例》有關條文的枝節性或技術性問題作出更為詳細的規定。

三、緊急立法的特殊功能

香港特區行政長官緊急立法權的功能，除了具有上文所述的緊急立法的一般功能之外，還具有如下特別功能。相較於一般功能，香港特區行政長官緊急立法的特殊功能更為宏觀。

（一）填補法制漏洞

從《香港基本法》關於應對香港緊急情況的憲制安排來看，在緊急權的行使主體方面，全國人民代表大會常務委員會是香港緊急情況處理的合"憲"機關，然而，這並不代表全國人民代表大會常務委員會是唯一的合"憲"機關。[1] 就緊急情況危害的程度而言，《香港基本法》的條文僅規定了緊急情況"危及國家統一和安全"的程度，並未涉及香港本地安全受損的程度。就應急的具體事務而言，《香港基本法》對香港本地機關的權力進行劃分時，並未嚴格區分緊急性與日常性、特殊性與一般性，導致香港特

---

1 Hualing Fu and Xiaobo Zhai, "Two Paradigms of Emergency Power: Hong Kong's Liberal Order Meeting the Authoritarian State", *Hong Kong Law Journal*, volume 50, part 2, 2020, p. 489.

別行政區缺乏應對緊急情況的憲制依據。上述內容反映出《香港基本法》在設計香港特區緊急法制方面存在諸多漏洞，使香港特區在緊急情況出現時更容易處於風險之中，進一步而言，若緊急情況危害到香港安全穩定，那麼亦必然會危害到《香港基本法》本身。

其實，早有學者指出，由於香港特別行政區對該地區的法律和秩序負有主要責任，它應該擁有一些緊急權力，這看起來是合理的。[1] 事實上，香港的緊急權力得到了於 1991 年通過的《香港人權法案條例》的確認，該條例的第 5 條規定：當公共緊急情況威脅國家生存，且這種威脅被官方宣佈時，在緊急情況的嚴格要求範圍內，可以依法採取克減《香港人權法案條例》所規定權利的措施。《香港人權法案條例》在香港回歸後，仍然是有效的法律，據此，香港特區有權正式宣佈香港進入公共緊急狀態。[2] 香港特別行政區據此擁有除了《香港基本法》第 18 條第 4 款條文規定的由全國人民代表大會常務委員會行使的緊急權以外的緊急權。有學者把全國人民代表大會常務委員會擁

1　Yash Ghai, *Hong Kong's New Constitutional Order*, Hong Kong University Press, 1999, p. 447.

2　Hualing Fu and Xiaobo Zhai, "Two Paradigms of Emergency Power: Hong Kong's Liberal Order Meeting the Authoritarian State", *Hong Kong Law Journal*, volume 50, part 2, 2020, p. 492.

有的緊急權稱為外部緊急權，而香港特別行政區擁有的緊急權稱為內部緊急權。外部緊急情況和內部緊急情況是緊急制度的兩種範式：前者是基於異常的狀態，在這種這狀態下管理危機，很大程度上不是依賴法律規則，亦不用承擔憲法和法律責任；而後者是基於法治的概念，這種情況下應急權要受到法律的約束。[1] 法治乃香港的核心價值之一。在當前背景下，《緊急條例》賦予行政長官會同行政會議行使緊急立法權很大程度上就能填補香港特區緊急法制的漏洞，為應對緊急情況、保障本地安全起到重要的保障作用。

（二）豐富應急措施

香港特別行政區政治體制的設計充分考慮了香港的歷史與現實，吸收了當代西方國家政治體制的一些良好元素，混合制的特徵十分明顯。然而，此種政治體制設計的出發點和基礎是回歸後香港能夠保持和平穩定的發展狀態，而對於應對香港可能出現的緊急情況顯然準備不足，"修例風波"造成的惡劣影響就是典型的例子。由於現代社會在高速發展過程中很容易出現各種類型的危機，尤其是社會上存在政治嚴重對立、社會出現撕裂、各種矛盾日

---

1 Ibid, p. 489.

益激化的時候，香港社會亦會面臨諸多潛在風險。而《香港基本法》在應對緊急情況的制度設計方面存在明顯不足，缺乏明確統一的應急制度，當危機出現時，就會表現出應急措施僵硬、簡單、滯後等不足，容易使社會秩序陷入混亂。在不違反《中國憲法》和《香港基本法》的前提下，通過《緊急條例》授予行政長官緊急立法權，可增強香港特區政府的應急能力，使其能及時有效處理危機，恢復社會秩序，維護香港的穩定繁榮。《緊急條例》授予行政長官的緊急立法權，豐富了香港特區政府應對緊急情況的措施，能有效降低緊急情況的危害程度，是香港保持長期穩定繁榮的有力保障。

（三）拓展彈性空間

"一國兩制"順利實施的前提是香港保持繁榮穩定，其中行政長官是連接中央與香港特別行政區的重要角色。若香港能總體保持平穩發展，即使過程中出現一些小的阻礙，中央政府對"一國兩制"的未來還是有信心的。然而，香港特區政府在高度自治下遇到緊急情況時，如果無法及時有效地應對處理，比如發生"修例風波"等一系列危害香港法治和國家安全的惡劣事件，則可能出現"政府失能、社會失序"的危險。如果香港特區政府無法擺脫困局，那麼最後的結果只能是由中央政府出手干預，這就可能造成香港特區的高度自治受到嚴重影響，對"一國兩制"產生難以預測的消極影響。如何避免陷入此種潛在危機？必須通過法律賦予香港特區行政長官行使緊急立法權，使得香港在應對緊急情況時多一把利器，這有利於鞏固"一國兩制"的基礎，擴展香港特區在"一國兩制"下應對緊急情況的彈性空間。[1]

1　底高揚：《論香港特別行政區行政長官的緊急立法權》，載《港澳研究》2021 年第 2 期，第 23-26 頁。

第三章　香港特區行政長官的緊急立法權與
行政主導體制

香港特別行政區的行政主導體制是指在司法獨立的情況下，行政長官及其領導的行政機關在香港特別行政區的權力分配和運行中，相對於立法機關而言處於優勢地位的一種政治體制。這種政治體制以權力分立為基礎，因此，它不是專制體制，而是民主體制。香港特區行政長官的緊急立法權，恰好與這種行政主導體制相契合。2019 年的社會暴亂對香港造成嚴重的損失，暴露了香港特區政府的應急能力確實存在不足，有必要通過賦予行政長官緊急立法權，來幫助香港特區政府及時高效地應對危機，恢復社會秩序，維護穩定繁榮。

第一節　香港特區的行政主導體制

關於香港特別行政區的政治體制所屬的類型，長期以來存在行政主導、三權分立的爭議。其實，香港特別行政區政治體制無疑屬於行政主導，亦具有權力分立的特徵，兩者高度統一於香港特別行政區的政治體制之中。

一、香港特區行政主導體制的內涵解析

"行政主導"是一個常見的概念，學者對其有不同的解讀。楊建平認為，行政主導可以從政權組織形式和政權運作方式兩個角度來認識：前者是指從國家政治權力分配的角度出發，行政機關相比其他政治機關在憲制層面上具有主導地位，此即"行政主導體制"；後者是從國家政治權力執行的角度出發，行政機關比其他政治機關在社會管理的過程中處於決策地位，就是真正的"行政主導"。[1]行政主導作為政權運作方式不限於行政主導體制，議會主導體制因政黨政治的作用，其政權運作方式亦會呈現行政

1　楊建平：《論香港實行行政主導的客觀必然性》，載《中國行政管理》2007年第 10 期，第 82 頁。

主導。

《香港基本法》第 4 章的標題就是"政治體制",其實涉及香港特別行政區的政治體制的制度規範還包括其他內容。總結起來,主要有如下幾個方面。

(一)關於行政長官的制度規範

第一,行政長官的法律地位。依據《香港基本法》第 43 條和第 60 條的規定,行政長官具有雙重法律身份,既是香港特別行政區的首長,對外代表特別行政區,又是特別行政區政府的首長,領導特別行政區政府。這說明行政長官作為特別行政區的首長,其法律地位比香港立法會主席及終審法院首席法官都要高。在此意義上說,行政長官可以作為香港特別行政區憲政秩序的維護者。有學者把香港特別行政區的行政主導體制稱為行政長官制,[1] 這亦未嘗不可。

第二,行政長官的職權。《香港基本法》第 48 條賦予行政長官在行政、人事、財政和立法等方面的廣泛職權,包括:領導香港特區政府;負責執行《香港基本法》和依照該法適用於香港特別行政區的其他法律;簽署立法會通過的法案,公佈法律;簽署立法會通過的財政預算案,將

1　王磊:《香港政治體制應當表述為"行政長官制"》,載《政治與法律》2016 年第 12 期,第 53-66 頁。

財政預算、決算報中央人民政府備案；決定政府政策和發佈行政命令；提名並報請中央人民政府任命主要官員；建議中央人民政府免除主要官員的職務；依照法定程序任免各級法院法官；依照法定程序任免公職人員；執行中央人民政府就《香港基本法》規定的有關事務發出的指令；代表香港特區政府處理中央授權的對外事務和其他事務；批准向立法會提出有關財政收入或支出的動議；根據安全和重大公共利益的考慮，決定政府官員或其他負責政府公務的人員是否向立法會或其屬下的委員會作證和提供證據；赦免或減輕刑事罪犯的刑罰；處理請願，申訴事項。這些法定職權支撐起行政長官崇高的法律地位，並便於行政長官依法施政。

第三，行政長官產生辦法。行政長官不是由立法會選舉產生，而是由一套獨立於立法會議員選舉方法之外的辦法來選出。因為行政長官和立法會的產生辦法相互獨立，"所以，理論上說，行政長官在政治上無須倚賴立法會議員或他們的選民，從而也不大受到他們的掣肘"[1]。為了完善香港特別行政區選舉制度，發展適合香港特別行政區

---

1 劉兆佳：《行政主導的政治體制 —— 設想與現實》，載中央人民政府駐香港特別行政區聯絡辦公室：《關於"一國兩制"和香港問題的理論文集》，第283頁。

實際情況的民主制度，2021 年 3 月 11 日第十三屆全國人民代表大會第四次會議通過《全國人民代表大會關於完善香港特別行政區選舉制度的決定》，該決定第 2 條規定，香港特別行政區設立一個具有廣泛代表性、符合香港特別行政區實際情況、體現社會整體利益的選舉委員會。選舉委員會負責選舉行政長官候任人、立法會部分議員，以及提名行政長官候選人、立法會議員候選人等事宜。選舉委員會由工商、金融界，專業界，基層、勞工和宗教等界，立法會議員、地區組織代表等界，香港特別行政區全國人大代表、香港特別行政區全國政協委員和有關全國性團體香港成員的代表界等五個界別共 1,500 名委員組成。行政長官的新選舉制度延續了《香港基本法》最初的附件一的理念，最大程度上減少了立法會議員對行政長官施政的掣肘。

此外，從 2002 年 7 月 1 日起，香港建立起高官問責制。在高官問責制下，主要官員在其負責範疇事宜內出現失誤時須承擔全部責任，甚至在出現嚴重失誤時要下臺。他們亦可能因嚴重的個人操守問題或不再符合《香港基本法》的有關規定而離職。主要官員之間沒有隸屬關係，全部由行政長官挑選，直接向行政長官負責。其中十一位政策局局長，除了公務員事務局局長必須來自公務員系統外，其餘都可由非公務員出任。在該制度下，有需要保留決策局的首長級薪級第 8 點（D8）公務員職位，他們會向相關的問責制主要官員負責。他們為決策局的工作所需承擔責任的方式及性質，與問責制局長不同，他們會協助局長管理政策局及部門，並會繼續出席公開場合，包括出席立法會事務委員會和其它委員會會議及接受傳媒採訪，出任這些職位的官員將改稱為"常任秘書長"。高官問責制無疑增強了行政長官對政府的領導力度，亦提高了依法施政的效率，是促進行政主導體制實施的有力舉措。

（二）行政與立法關係的制度規範

香港特別行政區行政主導體制主要體現在以行政長官及其領導的政府與立法會的關係上，前者的權力相對於後者的權力處於優勢地位。主要體現如下：

其一，行政長官及行政機關在立法中處於主動地位。《香港基本法》第 62 條第 5 項規定，特別行政區政府擬訂並提出法案、議案，由行政長官向立法會提出，政府擁有的立法創議權是行政主導的一大體現；《香港基本法》第 72 條第 2 項規定，政府提出的議案應當優先列入立法會議程，體現了行政優先；《香港基本法》第 74 條規定，立法會議員個人或聯名可提出不涉及公共開支、政治體制或政府運作的法案，凡涉及政府政策，在提出前必須得到行政長官的書面同意；立法會通過的法案須經行政長官簽署、公佈，方能生效，行政長官有權拒絕簽署法案，發回立法會重議。此外，《香港基本法》第72條第5項規定，行政長官有權在必要時要求立法會主席召開立法會緊急會議。

其二，《香港基本法》附件二還為立法會規定了一個獨特的投票機制，該機制有利於政府提出法案的通過。最初的附件二第2條第2款規定，政府提出的法案要求獲得出席會議的全體議員的簡單多數票通過，而由立法會成員個人提出的議案、法案以及對政府法案的修正案則需要功能團體選舉產生的議員和分區直接選舉、選舉委員會選舉產生的議員兩部分出席會議議員分別以簡單多數票通過。在設計香港特別行政區政治體制時，有人就建議採用兩院制，雖然該建議最後沒有被採納，但"一會兩組"的投票機制實現了兩院制的部分效果。在這種表決制下，政府提出的法案明顯比個人提出的法案容易通過；而對於個人提出的法案，有時即使得到多數人的支持，在"一會兩組"機制下亦有可能很難通過。"事實上，回歸以來，只有極為少數的議員議案和對政府提案的修正案能在立法會的會議上得以通過。可以說，分組投票的機制是成功地'捍衛＇了特別行政區的行政主導。＂[1] 此＂一會兩組＂的制度安排對政府十分有利 —— 它很容易阻止反政府法案的通過，是特區政府和建制派議員與反對派議員博弈的有效工具，比較有利於行政主導體制的運作。

其三，行政長官在一定條件下可以解散立法會。《香港基本法》第 50 條規定，香港特區行政長官如拒絕簽署立法會再次通過的法案或立法會拒絕通過政府提出的財政預算案或其他重要法案，經協商仍不能取得一致意見，行政長官可解散立法會。行政長官在解散立法會前，須徵詢行政會議的意見。雖然根據《香港基本法》第 73 條第 9 項的內容，立法會可以彈劾行政長官，但立法會只是提出彈劾案並報中央政府批准，行政長官最終能否被彈劾掉是由中央政府決定。此外，立法會彈劾對象僅限於行政長官，不包括政府主要官員。

其四，《香港基本法》等規範性法律文件對立法會及其議員權力的行使作出嚴格限制，這些受限的權力包括：（1）提出動議權。根據《香港基本法》第 48 條第 10 項，行政長官有權批准向立法會提出有關財政收入或支出的動議。根據《立法會議事規則》第 18 條，在每次會議中，

1　程介南：《對基本法政治體制的探討》，載蕭蔚雲：《香港基本法的成功實踐》，北京：北京大學出版社 2000 年版，第 42-43 頁。

政府提出的動議案，其處理上的優先次序高於議員提出的議案。（2）提案權。根據《香港基本法》第 74 條，凡不涉及公共開支或政治體制或政府運作者，可由立法會議員個別或聯名提出。凡涉及政府政策的法律草案，立法會議員在提出前必須得到行政長官的書面同意。（3）質詢權。根據《香港基本法》第 48 條第 11 項，行政長官決定政府官員或其他負責政府公務的人員是否向立法會或其屬下的委員會作證和提供證據。

總之，香港特別行政區的行政主導體制是指在司法獨立的情況下，行政長官及其領導的行政機關在香港特別行政區的權力分配和運行中，相對於立法機關而言處於優勢地位的一種政治體制。

二、香港特區行政主導體制的民主性

關於香港特別行政區的政治體制，亦有學者認為是權力分立體制，並否認行政主導。[1] 其實，權力分立與行政主導不是處於同一層面的事物，而是從不同角度對一國家（地區）政體特徵的描述。兩者的關係不是水火不容的，而是可以高度統一於同一國家（地區）政體之中。

1　陳祖為：《解釋〈基本法〉護法轉調　行政主導非〈基本法〉立法原意》，載《明報》2004 年 6 月 28 日。

之所以說香港特別行政區政體屬於權力分立體制，是因為這種政體符合權力分立的分權、制衡兩項要求。前文闡述了香港特別行政區行政主導體制的法制基礎，作為一種權力分立的體制，其亦有法制依據。香港特別行政區的管治權來源於中央的授予，根據《香港基本法》第四章"政治體制"的有關規定，香港特別行政區本地的管治權大體可分為行政[1]、立法和司法三個方面，此三權分別由行政長官為首的政府、立法會和法院行使。在司法獨立的情況下，行政與立法之間相互制衡。一方面，行政能夠制約立法。根據《香港基本法》第 48 條第 3 項的規定，行政長官簽署立法會通過的法案，公佈法律。立法會通過的法案必須經行政長官簽署、公佈，方能生效；根據《香港基本法》第 49 條的規定，行政長官對立法機關通過的法律有相對否決權；根據《香港基本法》第 50 條的規定，在一定情況下行政長官可以解散立法會。另一方面，立法亦能夠制約行政。根據《香港基本法》第 64 條的規定，特別行政區政府向立法會負責，執行立法會通過並已生效的法律，定期向立法會作施政報告，答覆立法會議員的質詢，徵稅和公共開支須經立法會批准；根據《香港基本

1　此處的行政權包括行政長官的權力和行政機關的權力，下同。

法》第 73 條第 9 項的規定，立法會可以彈劾行政長官。當然，香港特區的行政、立法和司法三權並非處於平衡狀態，在制度設計上，行政權處於相對優勢，但我們不能因為三權之間制約不平衡而否定香港特別行政區政體屬於分權體制。其實，即使是完全以權力分立為政體設計原則的國家，其立法、行政和司法三權亦並非都是處於平衡狀態，平衡只是理想追求，現實很難實現。就是實行權力分立最典型的美國，總統的權力亦相對國會的權力、聯邦法院的權力處於優勢地位。

當然，在香港特別行政區，除了本地的行政、立法和司法等權力外，還有中央政府的權力 —— 依據《香港基本法》第 13 條的外交權、依據第 14 條的防務權、依據第 15 條的行政長官等官員的任免權，等等。然而，並不會因此而不能討論香港特區政治體制所屬的類型。學界所說的香港特別行政區政治體制的類型或特徵，是探討香港本地行政、立法和司法等政權機關之間的關係，特別是它們之間的權力關係，並不涉及中央的權力。權威觀點亦認為香港特別行政區的政治體制包含"三權分置"的元素[1]，這

---

1 《關於香港特別行政區實行"三權分立"的說法必須糾正》，https://baijiahao.baidu.com/s?id=1677191744097493624&wfr=spider&for=pc（最後登錄日期：2022 年 10 月 3 日）。

亦是基於本地政權機關之間的權力關係得出的結論。"三權分置"不是新的概念，通常指中國內地農村土地所有權、承包權、經營權，既存在整體效用，又有各自功能，實施三權分置的重點是放活經營權。現在官方機構用此詞來形容香港的政治體制，以區別於西方的"三權分立"制度。主張香港特別行政區政治體制包含"三權分置"的元素者亦承認，行政與立法之間存在制衡關係，不否認司法獨立。[1] 既然公權力被分為行政、立法和司法三種，行政與立法之間存在相互制衡，司法保持獨立，這就是屬於分權體制。由此可見，權威觀點亦不否認香港特別行政區的政治體制是分權體制。

　　權力分立首先強調權力的來源和配置問題，其次才強調各權力之間的關係（制衡）問題。而行政主導主要是強調行政權相對立法權處於優勢地位，其實是探討行政權與立法權關係問題，是在分權所探討問題基礎上就行政權與立法權哪一個處於優勢地位所展開的進一步追問，故分權是主導的前提。正如張定淮教授所說："當代國家的主導權力絕大多數是建立在分權的基礎上的，甚至可以說沒有分權，就也無所謂主導，有分權才有誰佔主導的問題。"

1　同上。

這亦決定了香港特別行政區的行政主導不可能是行政主宰，更不可能是行政專制。香港的行政主導體制有一定的歷史淵源，回歸前的政治體制亦可被稱為"行政主導體制"，但那時的"行政主導體制"是專制體制，與回歸後的行政主導體制存在根本區別。

第二節 香港特區行政長官緊急立法權與 行政主導體制的契合

《香港基本法》確立的政治體制是行政主導的體制，該法的制定者就是要賦予行政長官較多的權力，以使行政長官及其領導的特區政府的權力相對於立法會的權力處於優勢地位。因此，《緊急條例》賦予行政長官緊急立法權符合《香港基本法》賦予行政長官更多權力的立法原意。行政長官的緊急立法權滿足應對緊急情況的需要，是香港保持穩定繁榮之必須。

一、賦予行政長官緊急立法權符合基本法的立法原意

如前所述，香港特別行政區的政治體制就是以行政長官為核心的行政主導體制，行政長官具有雙重法律地位，並具有非常廣泛的權力。這種行政主導體制的確立主要基於以下三方面的原因：其一，行政主導體制有利於維護國家主權。從 1985 年開始，港英就在香港推行激進的代議制民主改革，企圖建立一種立法主導的政治體制，以符合英方的最大利益。這種立法主導體制不僅不是維護國家主

權和領土安全的最好選擇，而且在香港複雜的政治生態下，還可能給國家主權和領土完整帶來危害。於是中方堅持在香港建立行政主導體制，"行政主導正是體現和維護國家主權的必要形式"。其二，行政主導體制便於實現中央政府領導。"強調行政主導是與肯定中央政府對香港的權力相關的。"[1] 在香港行政、立法、司法等政權機關中，只有行政長官及其領導的行政機關可以成為貫徹中央政府意旨的政權機關。這樣，"在行政主導體制下，行政機關對立法機關處於主動地位，不僅對立法機關具有很大的獨立性，而且還影響甚至主導了立法機關的行為。在權力的運行上，與立法機關一般不存在隸屬關係的狀況不同，下級行政機關更容易接受上級行政機關的影響。因此，在地方實行行政主導體制，有利於中央對地方的管控，有利於維護國家的最高意志"[2]。其三，行政主導體制能夠提高管治效率。在起草基本法之前，中方就認識到行政主導體制適合香港的實際情況，有利於實行高效率的行政管理，保持穩定繁榮。就香港的實際情況而言，香港是一個國際金融中心、航道中心、貿易中心和旅遊中心，經濟環境瞬息

1　陳弘毅：《香港特別行政區的法治軌跡》，北京：中國民主法制出版社 2010 年版，第 246 頁。

2　楊建平：《論香港實行行政主導的客觀必然性》，載《中國行政管理》2007 年第 10 期，第 80 頁。

萬變，這要求行政部門能適時提出立法建議或動議，立法機關按立法程序配合立法，這樣才能應付急劇變化的環境，實現有效管治。實行行政主導，就是保障特別行政區政府快速決策，提高管治效率，以適應香港社會管治和國際化都市的經濟發展需要。正如學者指出的，香港"內外交往頻繁，資訊靈通，商業、金融和其他行業的活動以及政治、文化各方面的問題錯綜複雜，瞬息萬變……更需要一個決策及時、效率較高、運作平穩、起主導作用的行政體制"。當然，以上三方面原因並不是完全割裂的，而是存在密切關係。

賦予行政長官緊急立法權加強了行政長官的權力，從而符合《香港基本法》實行行政主導體制的立法原意。如前所述，《香港基本法》第 18 條第 4 款僅規定了"危及國家統一和安全"程度的緊急情況，而緊急情況或緊急狀態還包括地震、海嘯等自然災害和暴亂等社會事件，因此，就應急的具體情況而言，香港特別行政區缺乏應對緊急情況的專門法律規範，《香港基本法》在此方面存在漏洞。《緊急條例》賦予行政長官非常廣泛的緊急立法權：（1）訂立涉及限制人身自由等十多種情形的規例的權力，而且任何規例或依據該規例訂立的命令或規則，即使與任何成文法則中所載者有抵觸，仍具效力；（2）所訂立的規例可就任何罪行規定以任何刑罰及制裁（包括強制性終身監禁的最高刑罰，但不包括死刑）；（3）任何人如違反任何根據《緊急條例》訂立的規例，而該等規例並無規定其他刑罰或懲罰，則可處第 2 級罰款及監禁 2 年。《緊急條例》賦予行政長官的這些緊急立法權，進一步豐富和加強了行政長官的權力。《緊急條例》賦予行政長官緊急立法權來應對這些突發緊急情況，恰好是對《香港基本法》賦予行政長官權力的必要補充，有效填補了法律漏洞。

賦予行政長官緊急立法權符合《香港基本法》的立法原意的另一體現，是行政長官具有緊急立法權可以保障行政主導體制得以實施。雖然《香港基本法》確定的政治體制是行政主導體制，但是行政長官施政曾長期受到立法會反對派多種形式的掣肘，政府施政舉步維艱，這種行政主導很大程度上僅僅停留在文本上，實踐中行政長官依法施政不順，有時甚至是寸步難行。在很長時期內，立法會一些反對派議員“為了反對而反對”，就是建制派的議員在民生經濟問題上，有時亦扮演過反對的角色。香港特區政府提出的立法議案在立法會曾屢次遭到“拉布”，而難以通過。雖然香港立法會在 2021 年實行新選舉制度後，立法會裏的議員分佈情況發生了決定性改變，政府提出的法案不會遭致“拉布”等阻撓，但政府法案在立法會審議必須經過"三讀"程序,難以滿足應對緊急情況的需要。另外,即使在實行新選舉制度下的香港立法會,通過選舉產生的議員、尤其是通過分區直選產生的議員,如果一味地支持特區政府,亦會面臨認受性降低的風險,因此他們亦要通過制約政府來"秀"自己的敬業精神。張炳良教授認為,目前由親政府政黨控制的立法會與行政長官和其他政治官員的較量不會比以前少,因此難以形成穩定的行政和立法關係。[1]立法會議員鄧飛的經歷證實了張炳良教授的上述觀點。鄧飛議員說,現任香港特區立法會議員善於提問、問答或會見政府官員討論政策問題,有時會提出尖銳的問題。立法會議員試圖監督政府的原因是,無論他們是由地方選區、功能界別或選舉委員會委員選舉產生的,他們都有強烈的動機向選民證明他們正在做積極的工作。[2]故此,鑒於香港特區行政長官施政仍然會受到來自立法會的強有力的制約,賦予行政長官緊急立法權,有利於消解行政主導體制運作過程中遇到的障礙,並可以最大化提高立法效率,以應對緊急情況,處理管治危機。行政機關作為社會管理的主要機關,不僅要承擔正常狀態下的公共事務

---

1 張炳良教授在 2022 年 6 月 18 日舉行的"紀念《基本法》實施 25 週年研討會:《基本法》理論研究的回顧與展望"上的演講。

2 朱世海與鄧飛議員在 2022 年 6 月 12 日的座談記錄。

管理，而且亦要承擔緊急情況下的危機管理。由此可見，行政主導體制的確立並不以緊急狀態的出現為前提，但是緊急狀態的消除卻十分依賴政府及時採取強有力的措施，以避免公民權利和社會秩序受到嚴重威脅。

二、賦予行政長官緊急立法權是保持香港穩定繁榮之必需

（一）行使緊急立法權及時高效地應對社會危機

緊急立法權的特性是及時高效應對危機的不二選擇。當國家處於緊急狀態時，社會的秩序和人民生命財產安全受到威脅，國家只有及時高效地採取應急措施，才能消除緊急狀態。為了及時有效地應對緊急狀態，恢復社會秩序，鑒於行政機關在處理國家具體管理事務方面較之立法機關、司法機關的天然優勢，行政機關常常被賦予較之國家常態下更多、更具強制性的應急權力。將國家正常狀態下屬於立法機關、司法機關的權力轉由行政機關行使，行政機關因此獲得眾多的手段來應對緊急狀況，其中最核心、最得力的手段就是行政緊急立法權。由於立法機關的立法具有滯後性，而緊急狀態具有突發性、複雜性和不可預測性，兩者的特性經常造成行政機關在採取應急措施時缺乏相關的法律依據，應急措施的合法性受到質疑，甚至

因此遭到民眾激烈反對而無法實施，嚴重影響了行政機關應急處理的效率和效力。行政緊急立法權讓行政首長獲得合法授權，可以針對具體的緊急情況，通過先訂立後審議的方式進行及時高效的立法，使得應急措施能得以實施，有利於儘快恢復社會秩序，亦充分體現了行政機關作為應急處理的指揮和決策機關中心，應該承擔起的應急管理的任務和責任。

緊急立法權的行使是現代管理的需要。隨著經濟的全球化和一體化，世界各地的經濟往來越來越頻繁，特別是作為世界經濟貿易中心的城市，跟世界經濟發展同呼吸共命運。而世界經濟發展的不平衡以及價值觀的衝突，導致了人類社會矛盾衝突越來越多，其體現是動亂和恐怖事件的頻發。另外，人類活動對自然環境的破壞也導致自然災難頻繁發生。作為經濟中心的大城市更容易發生上述緊急情況，因此世界很多國家都制定了相對完善的緊急狀態法來應對緊急情況的發生。然而，無論是採取制定統一的緊急法的方式，還是採取制定分散的針對具體某項緊急狀態的方式，都未必能妥善處理每次的緊急情況，例如統一的緊急法需要針對具體的緊急情況制定實施的細則，而分散式的緊急法更是需要每次重新制定具體的應急法律。為了彌補上述兩種緊急立法方式的不足，世界各國的主流做法是採取緊急立法的形式，即通過法律授予行政機關或行政首長緊急立法權，使其有權制定緊急法，使得行政應急措施合法化，保證行政機關能及時高效地應對危機，儘快恢復社會秩序，保障公民權利。

香港作為世界矚目的經濟貿易中心和現代化城市，亦會遭遇上述的緊急情況的問題，通過賦予香港特區行政長官緊急立法權來應對緊急情況，是符合世界各國的主流做法，亦契合香港目前的政治體制。香港位居東南亞戰略要衝以及中國內地和世界聯繫的重要樞紐，作為一個開放自由的國際化都市，受各種政治背景直接或間接影響的團體、機構和輿論工具相雜並存，人員構成複雜，一直存在各種活動猖獗的敵對勢力，存在危害國家和香港根本利益的破壞力量，並且被境外反華勢力當作向中國內地滲透的橋頭堡。香港是一個國際金融中心、航道中心、貿易中心和旅遊中心，經濟環境瞬息萬變，這又要求行政部門能適時提出立法建議或動議，立法機關按立法程序配合立法，這樣才能應付急劇變化的環境而實現有效管治。[1] 香港擁有約八百萬人口，面積相對狹小，總面積約 1,103 平方公里，而且資源大多依賴進口，如果資源的供給受到制約，社會

1　范振汝：《香港特別行政區的選舉制度》，香港：三聯書店（香港）有限公司 2006 年版，第 19 頁。

就容易產生動盪。由此可見，對於香港這樣的被經濟、政治、人口與資源緊張所困擾的國際化大都市，極易引發緊急情況。香港特別行政區政治制度和應急制度的選擇，主要是從香港的實際出發，行政主導體制和行政長官緊急立法權制度均適應這種對效率的"偏愛"：實行行政主導體制，就是保障特別行政區政府快速決策，提高管治效率，以適應香港社會管治和國際化都市的經濟發展需要；行政長官緊急立法權可以保障香港特區政府在處理緊急狀態時有更大的空間發揮作用，提高應急的效率和合法性，最大限度保障香港的穩定繁榮。正如一學者指出的，香港內外交往頻繁，資訊靈通，商業、金融和其他行業的活動以及政治、文化各方面的問題錯綜複雜……更需要一個決策及時、效率較高、運作平穩、起主導作用的行政體制。[1]香港特區行政長官具有緊急立法權，高度契合行政主導體制。

（二）香港特區行政長官行使緊急立法權能夠及時高效地維護穩定繁榮

這裏的穩定，主要是指社會穩定；繁榮，主要指經濟繁榮。穩定與繁榮之間存在相互促進的關係，穩定為繁榮提供基礎條件，而繁榮又會促進穩定。鄧小平在 1984 年

1　楊奇：《香港概論》（下），香港：三聯書店（香港）有限公司 1993 年版，第 44 頁。

會見港澳同胞國慶觀禮團時說："今後十三年和十三年以後保持香港的繁榮和穩定"[1]。由此，"保持香港繁榮穩定"就成為習慣性說法。鑒於沒有穩定不可能有繁榮，故筆者主張把穩定置於繁榮之前，以強調穩定與繁榮之間的邏輯關係。

2019 年注定是香港歷史上明珠黯淡的一頁，社會的動盪不安讓香港廣大市民迄今心有餘悸，暴亂對香港社會穩定繁榮的破壞力影響至今。此次事件的導火索是香港特區政府因應 "陳同佳案" 需要，於 2019 年 4 月向香港特區立法會提交了《逃犯條例》修訂草案，自 2019 年 6 月開始，香港的部分反對派和一些激進勢力不斷藉和平遊行集會之名，進行各種各樣激進的抗爭活動，反對立法會通過《逃犯條例》修訂草案。2019 年 10 月 23 日，《逃犯條例》修訂草案被撤回，但香港街頭的激進抗爭活動不但沒有結束，反而升級為暴亂。大量暴徒無視法律，以蒙面的方式繼續變本加厲地實施暴力破壞，導致香港許多銀行、店鋪、商場、學校以及地鐵等被打砸搶燒，破壞程度十分嚴重，香港亦因此連續數日幾乎陷入 "全城混亂" 和 "全城癱瘓" 的危險狀態。為了儘快平息暴亂、重建香港法治

---

1 《鄧小平文選》(第三卷)，北京：人民出版社 1993 年版，第 72 頁。

權威和依法恢復社會秩序，2019 年 10 月 4 日，時任香港特區行政長官林鄭月娥對外宣佈，她已經會同行政會議作出了決定，根據香港《緊急條例》第 1 條的規定訂立《禁止蒙面規例》，該規例於 2019 年 10 月 5 日實施。

香港此次通過訂立和實施《禁止蒙面規例》來止暴治亂，雖然遭到一些市民的激烈反對，甚至被起訴到香港特區法院，但是其效果是積極和顯著的。此次的修例風波，亦讓香港市民充分認識到僅僅讓政府消極不作為是不能夠滿足大多數人權利實現的要求的，在防止政府權力濫用為非的前提下，必須讓政府的權力為了市民的福祉積極運作起來。其實，從"二戰"結束以來，越來越多國家或地區的行政機關開始改變過去消極被動的狀況，其法定權力不斷強化，議會授予的行政立法權不斷增多，委任立法大量出現，行政機關從而成為最為積極、活躍的政權機關。近年來應對恐怖主義、金融危機等需要，行政機關的權力又得到擴大的機會。與行政機關擴權形成鮮明對比的是，立法機關的權力明顯式微，"即便是採取立法主導（議會主導）政制模式的西方國家，行政權在實際權力運作層面上都是居於主導地位的，只是程度強弱不同而已"[1]。總之，

---

1 傅思明：《香港特別行政區行政主導政治體制》，北京：中國民主法制出版社 2010 年版，第 36 頁。

社會治理的需要及行政權的特點，決定了行政權擴張早已經成為很多國家或地區政制發展無法阻擋的潮流，而這個潮流和趨勢在緊急狀態下更加明顯。

香港此次社會暴亂造成的嚴重損失，暴露了香港特區政府的應急能力確實存在不足，行政主導體制需要一個更加強有力的工具來實施。通過維護和加強行政長官緊急立法權來制定相關的緊急法律，可以幫助香港特區政府及時高效地應對各類危機，及時恢復社會秩序，維護香港大多數市民的利益，也有利於香港特區政府樹立威信，提高香港市民對其施政措施以及香港行政主導體制的認可和支持。故此，行政長官緊急立法權加強了行政主導體制，能夠促進香港社會保持穩定與繁榮。

當然，賦予行政機關這種緊急立法權必然造成行政機關權力的強化，這種強化是一把雙刃劍：一方面它的正當行使能高效解除危機，另一方面它的行使經常要對公民權利進行克減，可能對民主原則造成僭越，對法治政府產生衝擊。因此，行政緊急立法權必須受到監督和制約，其制定的應急法律必須有日落條款，而且在立法會恢復工作以後，要及時接受立法會的審議，並為權利的克減提供相關的司法救濟途徑。

第四章

香港特區《緊急條例》的合「憲」性判辨

香港特區高等法院原訟庭認為《緊急條例》違"憲"，即《緊急條例》授權行政長官會同行政會議認為在"危害公安"的情況下訂立《緊急條例》不符合《香港基本法》的規定，但高等法院上訴庭否定了此種判斷。案件最後上訴到香港特區終審法院，在《緊急條例》是否合乎《香港基本法》的事宜上，終審法院維持上訴庭的裁判。

第一節　《緊急條例》授權立法的合 "憲" 性

香港特區高等法院原訟庭法官認為，就《緊急條例》賦權行政長官會同行政會議在 "危害公安"（public danger）的情況下訂立規例而言，該條例不符合《香港基本法》。[1] 本案中，香港特區行政長官依據《緊急條例》頒佈《禁止蒙面規例》是對緊急立法權的行使，《禁止蒙面規例》與通常的附屬立法不同。《香港基本法》規定，行政長官有權制定附屬立法。[2] 根據《釋義及通則條例》，附屬立法指根據任何條例或具有立法效力的任何公告，制定具體的規則、條例、命令、決議、通知、法院規則、細則或其他文書。[3] 可見，附屬立法是針對那些普遍的、沒有明確的實施細則的規例條例的立法，它必須是針對特定的規例條例。而行政長官行使緊急立法權制定的條例不同於一般附屬立法，因為緊急立法權往往不是對已有的具體法律或條例進行細化，而是針對危機制定新的規範。《緊急條

1　*Leung Kwok Hung v. Secretary for Justice and CEIC*, HCAL 2945, 2949/2019, para. 4.

2　《香港基本法》第 56 條。

3　《釋義及通則條例》第 3 條。

例》只為行政長官制定規例提供了權力基礎，而不是制定規例的規範基礎。因此，這類立法在一般意義上並不同於附屬立法，因為它並非對任何現有法律或規例的具體化。

原訟庭法官認為《緊急條例》授予或委託一般立法權給行政長官是違"憲"的，其主要原因有如下兩方面：一方面，從實質問題來看，根據《緊急條例》制定的法規很少是附屬立法，這表明《緊急條例》賦予了行政長官一般的立法權；另一方面，依《緊急條例》獲得的立法權不是制定附屬立法，而是制定主體法例（primary legislation）。[1]而香港現行的憲制性法律與回歸前不同，因此在回歸後，立法會不得授權行政長官行使一般立法權。[2]

筆者不同意原訟庭法官的上述意見。首先，就香港的憲制而言，在回歸之前，立法局並不是一個"主權"機構，更沒有最高權力，總督才是"主權者"英國國王的代表。回歸後，根據《香港基本法》，行政長官具有雙重法律地位，他／她不僅是香港特區的行政首長，而且亦是特區政府的負責人。作為行政長官，其地位高於其他政制機關。行政長官亦有必要擁有緊急立法權來應對疾病、自然

---

1 *Leung Kwok Hung v. Secretary for Justice and CEIC*, HCAL 2945, 2949/2019, para. 55.

2 Ibid.

災害、動亂等問題。第二，原訟庭法官認為行政長官依據《緊急條例》所獲得的立法權不是制定附屬立法，而是行使一般立法權。這涉及到對根據《緊急條例》制定的附屬立法的理解，這是一種"獨立附屬立法"。至於法官提到的立法程序問題，這是可以理解的，《釋義及通則條例》規定的是一般情況下的立法程序，它不能完全適用於緊急立法。第三，高等法院上訴庭和終審法院都認為，《緊急條例》授權行政長官會同行政會議制定的附屬規例不屬於主體法例。[1]高等法院上訴庭在對《緊急條例》的合"憲"性進行分析時，依賴連續性這一主題，並在詳細審查了該條例的主要特徵後，得出結論，認為《緊急條例》並未授予行政長官會同行政會議制定主體法例的一般立法權。[2]其實，根據《緊急條例》制定的附屬立法不是通常的附屬立法，而是"獨立附屬立法"，這種"獨立附屬立法"不是對上位法的細化，而是創制新的規則。

1　汪超：《表達自由的邊界與基本法的解釋：從香港三級法院〈禁蒙面法〉相關判決看香港基本法的本地適用》，載《法律適用》2021年第4期，第124頁。

2　*Leung Kwok Hung v. Secretary for Justice and CEIC*, FACV nos. 6, 7, 8 and 9 of 2020, [2020] HKCFA 42, para. 30.

第二節 緊急立法規定刑事處罰的合"憲"性

《緊急條例》規定，任何人如違反該等規例或香港現行法律，可被拘捕、審訊及懲罰，[1] 任何犯罪均可以判處最高終身監禁的刑罰。[2] 在原訟庭，原告主張《緊急條例》授權行政長官制定《禁止蒙面規例》限制了受《香港基本法》和《香港人權法案條例》保護的基本權利，這違反了《香港基本法》第 39 條的規定。[3] 原告認為，對權利的限制必須由已通過的法律規定，並由立法機關加以審查。[4] 香港特區高等法院原訟庭法官不同意上述觀點，並指出許多香港法規頒佈的時代並沒有民選的立法機關。[5] 法官還指出，普通法中對犯罪的審判判例亦可以構成一種"法律"，實現對基本權利限制。[6] 香港特區高等法院原訟庭法官贊成附屬法規可以限制基本權利的觀點，但亦認為根據《緊急條

1　《緊急條例》第 2 条第 2 款第 n 項。

2　《緊急條例》第 3 条第 1 款。

3　*Leung Kwok Hung v. Secretary for Justice and CEIC*, [2019] HKCFI 2820, para. 11.

4　Ibid, para. 118.

5　Ibid.

6　Ibid, para. 119.

例》規定，任何犯罪均最高可判處終身監禁的規定是非法的。[1] 法官的理由是該觀點違反了《釋義及通則條例》第 28 條第 1 款第 e 項關於附屬條例的規定，因為該法例規定，對違反附屬條例的罪行的最高刑罰為罰款 5000 港元或 6 個月監禁。[2]

筆者認為，根據《緊急條例》制定的附屬立法可以限制基本權利，甚至可以規定刑事責任，因為在英國等普通法國家和地區，行政立法亦可以規定犯罪、刑罰。然而，筆者亦認同原訟庭法官的看法，即《緊急條例》不宜規定對任何最高可達強制性終身監禁的罪行的懲罰。其原因並不是法官所說的那樣，即它違反了《釋義及通則條例》第 28 條第 1 款第 e 項所規定的附屬立法的規範。事實上，根據《緊急條例》制定的法規屬於"獨立附屬立法"，這與《釋義及通則條例》中的法規不同。歷史事實亦表明，根據《緊急條例》制定的附屬立法並不是《釋義及通則條例》中的附屬立法。1967 年，港英政府發佈了一系列緊急法令，以應對一場嚴重的騷亂，允許政府不經審判或提供理由，可將任何人拘留一年。與此同時，它還增加了地方法院的權力，授權它在處理與該騷亂有關的案件時，

1　Ibid, para. 67.

2　Ibid.

將最高刑期從五年增加到十年。[1]當時，港英政府頒佈的這些附屬立法顯然修改了現行的相關法律，並沒有遵守《釋義及通則條例》。如前所述，《香港基本法》中的附屬立法不僅包括《釋義及通則條例》中的一般附屬立法，還包括根據《緊急條例》制定的"獨立附屬立法"。正如香港特區高等法院原訟庭法官所說，《釋義及通則條例》並不直接適用於《香港基本法》規定的附屬立法、附屬法規，事實上附屬立法或附屬法規是在《香港基本法》生效後的 1998 年才添加到《釋義及通則條例》第 3 條。[2]《香港基本法》中"附屬立法"一詞的含義必須取決於一種自主的解釋，而不是在《釋義及通則條例》中隨後的定義。[3]這樣可以避免行政長官制定的附屬法規與《釋義及通則條例》的相關規定發生衝突。正如一位學者所說，法律不是上帝，而是人制定的，法律不可能是完美的。因此，發現法律的缺陷並不是一種成就，將有缺陷的法條解釋得沒有

1　葉建民：《回顧歷史：這個錯誤真的有用嗎？》，載《明報》2019 年 10 月 11 日。

2　《釋義及通則條例》第 3 條規定了附屬法例、附屬法規、附屬立法（subsidiary legislation, subordinate legislation），其內涵是指根據或憑藉任何條例訂立並具有立法效力的文告、規則、規例、命令、決議、公告、法院規則、附例或其他文書。

3　*Leung Kwok Hung v. Secretary for Justice and CEIC*, [2019] HKCFI 2820, para. 54.

缺陷才是智慧。[1] 普通法中有一個基本原則，即法律不得隨意廢除。因此，如果通過解釋可使兩種看似衝突的法律沒有衝突，法院應採用這種解釋。[2] 筆者認為，根據《緊急條例》制定的附屬法規可以規定最高可達強制性終身監禁的刑罰，明顯不當。香港的附屬立法可以規定刑事犯罪是來自英國的法制傳統。在英國，2010 至 2011 年附屬立法規定了 133 項刑事犯罪，但最高刑罰僅為五年監禁。[3]

綜上所述，筆者同意高等法院原訟庭法官的觀點，行政長官需要有效處理 "緊急情況" 和 "危害公安" 的情況。但是，在上述訴訟中，原告不同意行政長官的緊急立法權可以規定最高可達強制性終身監禁的刑罰，該意見得到法院的肯定。在理論界中，大家一致認為，刑法應該保持謙抑，特別是非常嚴厲的無期徒刑的懲罰。這亦是原訟庭判斷《緊急條例》違反了《香港基本法》的一個重要原因。筆者同意法院的觀點，即行政立法規定對個人自由的非常嚴厲的懲罰是不合適的。

1　張明楷：《法律不是被嘲笑的對象 —— 犯罪最大化的發展》，www.law-lib.com/flsz/sz_view.asp?no=2253（最後登錄日期：2020 年 3 月 18 日）。

2　陳文敏：《香港人權法案生效首年的回顧》，載《法學評論》1992 年第 4 期，第 77 頁。

3　James Chalmers and Fiona Leverick, "Criminal Law in the Shadows: Creating Offences in Delegated Legislation", *Legal Studies*, volume 38, 2018, p. 224.

第三節　緊急立法修改立法會立法的合"憲"性

《緊急條例》規定，行政長官會同行政會議可以修改任何成文法則，暫停任何成文法則的運作，並適用任何成文法則。[1] 如前所述，這一規定已招致香港法律界的批評，申請人亦已提出質疑。在香港特區高等法院原訟庭的判決中，法官同意申請人的觀點。其主要原因是，香港的憲政制度不允許立法會將該等權力授予行政長官，而《釋義及通則條例》規定，附屬立法不得與任何條例的條文相抵觸。[2] 對這個問題的討論與"亨利八世條款"相互聯繫。

在考察了英國的附屬立法後，筆者發現英國的附屬立法可以修改、廢除議會的立法，這是由英國領導的英聯邦法律體系的傳統。當涉及到通過附屬立法修改法律的可能性時，有必要參考"亨利八世條款"。"議會可以通過授權的立法，授予修改、暫停、推翻甚至廢除主體法例的權力"，這樣的法規制定條款通常被稱為"亨利八世條款"。[3]

1　《緊急條例》第 2 條第 2 款第 g 項。

2　《釋義與通則條例》第 28 条第 1 款第 b 項。

3　See Mary Harris and David Wilson, *Parliamentary Practice in New Zealand*, Auckland: Oratia Media Ltd, 2017, p. 465.

這一條款是根據 1539 年的公告法令而這樣命名的，該法令賦予了國王亨利八世通過公告立法的權力。[1] 這一條款很快被擴展到英聯邦的其他國家和地區。應該特別指出的是，根據"亨利八世條款"對現有法律的修正案是非常有限的。畢竟，該條款規定，授權立法允許政府對法律進行修改，而不需要推動通過一項全新的法案，最初的法案就有規定，允許未來的授權立法在不同程度上修改法律。[2] 此外，這些改變通常不是原則性的，而是技術性的。"這些變化範圍是從技術上的，比如改變罰款的水準，到更詳細地充實行為。"[3]

在《緊急條例》第 2 條第 2 款第 g 項中還有一個"亨利八世條款"，規定根據《緊急條例》制定的法規，可以修改或暫停任何成文法則的運行，或適用任何不論是否經過修改的成文法則。然而，香港特區高等法院原訟庭並沒有批准它，理由是在《香港基本法》中沒有任何條款授權行政長官自己修改或廢除主體法例。[4] 筆者對此有不同

1　See Mirko Pečarič, "An Old Absolutist Amending Clause as the 'New' Instrument of Delegated Legislation", *The Theory and Practice of Legislation*, volume 4, 2016, p. 5.

2　"Understanding UK Legislation", https://www.soas.ac.uk/library/subjects/law/research/file70251.pdf (last accessed on 8 December 2019).

3　Ibid.

4　*Leung Kwok Hung v. Secretary for Justice and CEIC*, [2019] HKCFI 2820, para. 64.

意見，從上面可以看出，"亨利八世條款"是存在於英國的。當然，反對者會指出，香港不是一個主權國家，無法與英國相比。事實上，這一條款亦存在於澳大利亞的昆士蘭州。在蘇格蘭（英國的一部分）亦有類似的案例，下位階的立法經常被用來：提供法律如何適用的細節；使法案的特定部分（或部分）生效；並修改現有的法案。[1] 由此可見，香港特區高等法院原訟庭的法官認為，"亨利八世條款"的有效性基礎是議會主權，[2] 這種看法是不正確的。"亨利八世條款"在上述國家和地區原則上被禁止使用，只能用於處理特殊事項。在香港，行政長官會同行政會議只能在"緊急情況"或"危害公安"的情況下，行使緊急立法權，這亦符合國際慣例。行政長官根據《緊急條例》制定的附屬立法屬於上述"獨立附屬立法"。雖然這種附屬立法是獨立的，但它不是一般的立法，因為它是在立法會的授權下制定的，這與英國的立法相同。在英國，根據《1998年人權法》第42條的目的，緊急條例應被視為附屬立法，而不是主體法例（無論它們是否修改主體法

---

1 "Subordinate Legislation", available at https://www.parliament.scot/visitandlearn/100539.aspx (last accessed on 27 November 2019).

2 *Leung Kwok Hung v. Secretary for Justice and CEIC*, CACV 541, 542 & 583/2019, para. 65.

例）。[1]同理，根據《緊急條例》作出的規例，甚至是根據該條例作出的命令或規則，即使在任何法令中所載的與該條例不一致的地方，均具有效力。[2]

《緊急條例》中屬於"亨利八世條款"的第 2 條第 2 款第 g 項規定，法令可以修改任何成文法，暫停任何成文法的運作。這表明，與英國的緊急狀態法相比，《緊急條例》顯然對"亨利八世條款"的適用缺乏限制和審查。一般來說，"亨利八世條款"只應例外使用，而不是定期使用，並應包括日落條款，即所制定的規定在一段時間後被廢除。[3]《緊急條例》授權行政長官僅在"緊急情況"和"危害公安"兩種情況下行使特殊立法權，但由於"緊急情況"和"危害公安"沒有定義，行政長官的自由裁量權特別大。根據《緊急條例》制定的附屬立法自動生效，不需要立法會的批准。此外，根據《緊急條例》制定的附屬立法的有效時間並沒有得到明確的定義，完全由行政長官決定。行政長官依據《緊急條例》訂立的法規能否修改或暫停《香港人權法案條例》的運作？筆者注意到根據英國

1　英國《國內緊急狀態法（2004）》第 23 條第 1 款。

2　《緊急條例》第 2 条第 4 款。

3　See Mirko Pečarič, "An Old Absolutist Amending Clause as the 'New' Instrument of Delegated Legislation", *The Theory and Practice of Legislation*, volume 4, 2016, p. 7.

《國民緊急應變法（2004）》制定的法規不得修改《1998年人權法》（c.42），故行政長官依據《緊急條例》制定的法規以不違反《香港人權法案條例》為宜。有學者已指出，應考慮到香港的附屬立法亦不能修改《香港人權法案條例》。[1] 因此，行政長官非常有必要嚴格規範"亨利八世條款"的立法，特別是要經立法會的審查，這不僅可以阻止行政長官的獨裁傾向，而且可以體現行政長官立法的民主性和合法性。

1　Jack Simson Caird, Robert Hazell and Dawn Oliver, *The Constitutional Standards of the House of Lords Select Committee on the Constitution*, the Constitution Unit in School of Public Policy, University College London, 2015, p. 8.

第四節　對《緊急條例》已被廢止觀點的分析

案件原告方提出，《香港人權法案條例》第 3 條第 2 款 "默示廢止" 了《緊急條例》。或完全廢除，或在不符合《香港人權法案條例》第 5 條的情況下廢除，或由《香港基本法》第 39 條所適用的《公民權利和政治權利國際公約》第 4 條廢除，這些都是《緊急條例》被 "默示廢止"（implied repeal）的理由。[1] 筆者對此不敢苟同。

《香港人權法案條例》第 3 條第 2 款規定，所有與《香港人權法案條例》不一致的現有法例均被廢除。《緊急條例》並沒有違反《香港人權法案條例》，亦沒有被廢止，港英立法局在 1993 年還對其第 3 條第 1 款進行修訂。根據《全國人民代表大會常務委員會關於根據〈中華人民共和國香港特別行政區基本法〉第 160 條處理香港原有法律的決定》，所有與《香港人權法案條例》不一致的現有法例均被廢除的規定不採用為香港特別行政區法律，《香港人權法案條例》在香港法律體系中不再具有凌駕性的地

1　*Leung Kwok Hung v. Secretary for Justice and CEIC*, FACV no. 8/2020, para. 14.

位。《香港人權法案條例》第 5 條規定：（1）如經當局正式宣佈緊急狀態，而該緊急狀態危及國本，得在此種危急情勢絕對必要之限度內，採取減免履行人權法案規定義務的措施，但採取此等措施，必須按照法律而行。（2）根據第 1 款採取之措施不得 ——（a）抵觸依國際法所負並適用於香港之義務，但依《公民權利和政治權利國際公約》所負之義務除外；（b）引起純粹以種族、膚色、性別、語言、宗教或社會階級為根據之歧視；或（c）減免履行人權法案第 2、3、4（1）及（2）、7、12、13 及 15 條之規定。依據上述規定，《緊急條例》亦沒有被"默示廢止"，因為《緊急條例》授予行政長官的緊急權沒有減免履行人權法案規定的義務。終審法院法官在判決書中亦指出，當《香港人權法案條例》於 1991 年生效時，《緊急條例》並沒有因不符合其第 3（2）條和第 5 條的規定而被廢止，因此，我們拒絕申請人的此論點。[1]

《公民權利和政治權利國際公約》第 4 條共有三款，分別規定：（1）如經當局正式宣佈緊急狀態，危及國本，本盟約締約國得在此種危急情勢絕對必之限度內，採取措施，減免履行其依本盟約所負之義務，但此種措施不得抵

1　Ibid, para. 79.

觸其依國際法所負之其他義務，亦不得引起純粹以種族、膚色、性別、語言、宗教或社會階級為根據之歧視。（2）第 6 條、第 7 條、第 8 條（第 1 款及第 2 款）、第 11 條、第 15 條、第 16 條及第 18 條之規定，不得依本條規定減免履行。（3）本盟約締約國行使其減免履行義務之權利者，應立即將其減免履行之條款，及減免履行之理由，經由聯合國秘書長轉知本盟約其他締約國。其終止減免履行之日期，亦應另行移文秘書長轉知。《公民權利和政治權利國際公約》第 4 條第 1 款已經被《香港人權法案條例》第 5 條落實。如前所述，依據《香港人權法案條例》第 5 條的規定，《緊急條例》並沒有被"默示廢止"。《公民權利和政治權利國際公約》第 6 條是關於死刑的規定，第 7 條是關於禁止酷刑、非經本人同意不得對任何人作醫學或科學試驗的規定，第 8 條第 1 款和第 2 款是關於禁奴的規定，第 11 條是關於禁止對因無力履行契約義務者予以監禁的規定，第 15 條是關於罪刑法定的規定，第 16 條是關於保障法律人格的規定，第 18 條是關於宗教信仰自由的規定，而依據《緊急條例》的立法對這些事項大多沒有涉及，或有所涉及但並沒有違反《公民權利和政治權利國際公約》的規定。因為香港特區政府沒有行使其減免履行《公民權利和政治權利國際公約》所規定義務之權利，所以《緊急條例》亦沒有違反《公民權利和政治權利國際公約》第 4 條第 3 款的規定。

第五節 香港特區法院對立法會立法的審查

香港特區高等法院原訟庭判決《緊急條例》授權行政長官會同行政會議在"危害公安"場合制定條例違"憲"，因此，根據《緊急條例》基於"危害公安"理由制定的《禁止蒙面規例》無效。[1] 此裁判意見，亦得到香港特區高等法院上訴庭的支持。該案件最後上訴到香港特區終審法院，終審法院認為《緊急條例》授權行政長官會同行政會議在"危害公安"場合制定條例符合《香港基本法》。香港特區高等法院原訟庭的裁判一作出，就引致中央有關部門的批評。香港特別行政區法院確實無權裁判《緊急條例》是否違"憲"。與此相關的問題是香港特別行政區法院對立法會立法是否具有審查權。

一、香港特區法院能否裁判《緊急條例》違"憲"？

香港特區高等法院原訟庭認為《緊急條例》賦予行政長官在某些情況下制定有關規例的規定，不符合《香港

---

1 *Leung Kwok Hung v. Secretary for Justice and CEIC*, HCAL 2945/2019, [2019] HKCFI 2884, para. 4.

基本法》。此做法得到香港特區高等法院上訴庭法官的支持，上訴庭的法官在裁判書中亦指出，在《香港基本法》的框架下，當法庭提出質疑時，有關法律的合"憲"性可通過立法程序或司法程序處理；而法庭有管轄權，亦確實有憲法責任這樣做以處理合"憲"性問題，如果發現情況屬實，則予以宣佈這樣的法律與《香港基本法》相抵觸。這樣做，法院不會違反《香港基本法》第160條，或以任何方式削弱全國人民代表大會常務委員會所作決定的權威。[1]

全國人民代表大會常務委員會法制工作委員會發言人在2019年11月19日就香港特區高等法院原訟庭有關司法覆核案判決發表如下談話：11月18日，香港特區高等法院原訟庭作出一項判決，其中裁定香港《緊急條例》部分條款不符合《香港基本法》，致使有關條款無效。一些全國人大代表對此表示強烈不滿，全國人民代表大會常務委員會法制工作委員會對此表示嚴重關切。《中國憲法》和《香港基本法》共同構成特別行政區的憲制基礎，香港特別行政區法律是否符合《香港基本法》，只能由全國人民代表大會常務委員會作出判斷和決定，任何其他機

1　*Leung Kwok Hung v. Secretary for Justice and CEIC*, CACV no. 541, 542 & 583/2019, para. 49.

118

關都無權作出判斷和決定。根據《香港基本法》第 8 條的規定，包括《緊急條例》在內的香港原有法律，除同本法相抵觸或經香港特別行政區立法機關作出修改者外，予以保留。1997 年 2 月 23 日，第八屆全國人民代表大會常務委員會第 24 次會議作出的《全國人民代表大會常務委員會關於根據〈中華人民共和國香港特別行政區基本法〉第 160 條處理香港原有法律的決定》，已經將《緊急條例》採用為香港特別行政區法律。因此，該條例是符合《香港基本法》的。香港特區高等法院原訟庭有關判決的內容嚴重削弱香港特區行政長官和政府依法應有的管治權，不符合香港《香港基本法》和全國人民代表大會常務委員會有關決定的規定。[1] 國務院港澳辦發言人亦在 2019 年 11 月 19 日就香港特區高等法院原訟庭有關《禁止蒙面規例》司法覆核案判決發表談話，對該判決產生的嚴重負面社會影響表示強烈關注。發言人表示，香港現行的《緊急條例》經過 1997 年 2 月全國人民代表大會常務委員會有關決定確認符合《香港基本法》，並採納為香港特別行政區法律，這表明該條例的全部規定都符合《香港基本法》。香港特

---

1 《香港"禁蒙面法"無效？全國人大、國務院港澳辦表態！》，https://www.163.com/dy/article/EUCRL2QN055040N3.html（最後登錄日期：2022年 10 月 12 日）。

區行政長官會同行政會議依據該條例制定《禁止蒙面規例》，即為依照《香港基本法》和全國人民代表大會常務委員會有關決定履行職權。該規例實施以來，對止暴制亂發揮了積極作用。高等法院原訟庭判決《緊急情況規例條例》賦予行政長官在某些情況下制定有關規例的規定不符合《香港基本法》，並裁決《禁止蒙面規例》的主要內容不符合相稱性標準，公然挑戰全國人民代表大會常務委員會的權威和法律賦予行政長官的管治權力，將產生嚴重負面社會政治影響。[1]

全國人民代表大會常務委員會於香港回歸時就明確了《緊急條例》符合《香港基本法》，並採用為特別行政區法律，在此情況下，香港特別行政區法院不應裁判《緊急條例》違"憲"，否則就有挑戰全國人民代表大會常務委員會權威的嫌疑。《香港基本法》第 160 條作了如下規定，從香港特別行政區成立時開始，香港原有的法律除了由全國人民代表大會常務委員會宣佈為與《香港基本法》抵觸者外，全部採用為香港特別行政區的法律規範，如果以後發現有法律與《香港基本法》抵觸的，可依照《香港基本法》規

---

1 《香港"禁蒙面法"無效？全國人大、國務院港澳辦表態！》，https://www.163.com/dy/article/EUCRL2QN055040N3.html（最後登錄日期：2022年 10 月 12 日）。

定的程序進行修改或停止生效。這說明，回歸時確認符合
《香港基本法》的原有法律，亦有可能在後來被發現不符合
《香港基本法》。因此，香港特別行政區法院可以對全國人
民代表大會常務委員會已經確認合乎《香港基本法》的本
地原有法律的合「憲」性提出質疑。其實，《香港基本法》
並沒有規定按什麼程序進行修改或停止生效。筆者主張，
如果法院發現某項法例（例如《禁止條例》）可能違反《香
港基本法》，就可向終審法院報告。如果終審法院亦認為此
法違反《香港基本法》，就把該法例提交到全國人民代表大
會常務委員會進行審查。全國人民代表大會常務委員會如
果認為該法例違反《香港基本法》，則將該法例發回香港立
法會，立法會按照有關程序予以修改或停止生效。

二、香港特區法院對立法會立法是否具有審查權？

香港特區高等法院原訟庭作出上述裁判引致中央有關
部門的嚴厲批評，與此相關的問題是香港特別行政區法院
對立法會立法是否具有審查權。對此問題全部肯定或全部
否定可能都不合適，需要分兩種情況解析。《香港基本法》
第 17 條規定，香港特別行政區享有立法權，由香港特別
行政區立法機關制定的法律須報全國人民代表大會常務委
員會備案，且備案不會影響該法律的生效。全國人民代表

大會常務委員會在徵詢其所屬的香港特別行政區基本法委員會後，如果認為香港特別行政區立法機關制定的任何法律不符合《香港基本法》關於中央管理的事務及中央與香港特別行政區的關係的條款，可將相關法律發回香港立法機關，但不作修改。經全國人民代表大會常務委員會發回的法律立即失效。除香港特別行政區的法律另有規定外，此法律的失效無溯及力。由《香港基本法》第 17 條的以上規定可看出，全國人民代表大會常務委員會對立法會立法的備案審查的範圍僅涉及中央管理的事務以及中央與香港特別行政區的關係。全國人民代表大會常務委員會不審查香港特區立法會立法中的特區自治範圍內的條款是否符合《香港基本法》，這不是立法者的疏漏，而是貫徹"一國兩制"的要求。[1] 假如全國人民代表大會常務委員會沒有把立法會立法發回，就視為全國人民代表大會常務委員會認為立法會立法合乎《香港基本法》。如果香港特別行政區法院在司法實踐中認為立法機關制定的法律不符合《香港基本法》中關於中央管理的事務以及中央與香港特別行政區的關係的條款，自然不能直接宣佈該法律不符合《香港基本法》，而是應按照上述程序，由終審法院提請全國

1　陳欣新：《香港與中央的"違憲審查"協調》，載《法學研究》2000 年第 4 期，第 141 頁。

人民代表大會常務委員會處理。對於立法會立法中的自治範圍內條款，香港特別行政區法院可以進行審查，並作出是否合乎《香港基本法》的裁判。當然，這是個長期存在爭議的問題，但在學界已有基本共識。香港特別行政區法院具有此權力的原因總結如下。

首先，在回歸之前，香港實行的是普通法制度，已經形成了由法院負責的司法審查制度。有學者指出："香港特區法院的司法權限顯然不能超越英國司法機關的司法權限範圍。英國司法機關所不擁有的違憲審查權，香港特區法院顯然從法理上也不能擁有。"[1]但實際情況並非如此。在回歸前，香港的法院可以根據英國發佈的憲法法律文件來審查本地的立法和行政行為。[2]特別是在 1991 年，港英政府通過了《香港人權法案條例》，其中規定雖然人權法是普通法，但它們被賦予了"憲法"的角色。當時，港英還將國際人權公約的條款複製到憲制法律文件中。通過1991 年的"R. v. Sin Yau Ming 案"，法院將違"憲"審查權的名稱置於之下。這個系統已經包含（或"潛伏"）了

1　董立坤、張淑鈿：《香港特別行政區法院的違反基本法審查權》，載《法學研究》2010 年第 3 期，第 13 頁。

2　Ann D. Jordan, "Lost in the Translation: Two Legal Cultures, the Common Law Judiciary and the Basic Law of the Hong Kong Special Administrative Region", *Cornell International Law Journal*, volume 30, p. 357.

一些機制性的"憲法審查"，也就是說，香港可根據憲法規範去裁判效力較低的法律規範的合理性或妥當性，而通過某些司法實踐，這種機制確實可以發展成"憲法審查"系統。[1] 在回歸後，香港特區法院的司法審查權有增無減，其適用範圍從公約的人權標準擴大到《香港基本法》的任何其他規定。[2]

其次，雖然《香港基本法》沒有明確授予香港特區法院審查立法會立法的權力，但保留了香港特區法院的原始管轄權，包括原來的普通法的法律解釋權。《香港基本法》第 11 條第 2 款規定，香港特別行政區立法機關制定的任何法律，均不得同本法相抵觸。這些規定可被理解為特別行政區法院行使違"憲"審查權的法律基礎。有必要強調的是，《香港基本法》第 158 條明確賦予法院在審理案件時解釋本法的權力。根據解釋權與審查權之間的邏輯關係，以及各國司法審查的實踐和經驗，可以推斷得出香港特別行政區法院有權根據《香港基本法》對立法會立法進行審查。換句話說，香港特別行政區法院根據《香港基本法》審查立法會立法的權力是《香港基本法》的"隱含

1　林來梵：《從規範憲法到憲法規範 —— 規範憲法學的一種前言》，北京：法律出版社 2001 年，第 395 頁。
2　陳弘毅：《香港的憲政發展：從殖民地到特別行政區》，載《洪範評論》第 12 輯，第 167 頁。

權力"。[1] 自香港回歸以來，特區法院已在數百起案件審理過程中對《香港基本法》作出司法解釋，其中許多案件是根據《香港基本法》賦予的"隱含權力"來審查政府的行政行為和立法會的立法行為。在本案件判決書中，香港特區法院亦指出，自香港特別行政區成立以來，香港特區法院在行使《香港基本法》第 19 條和《香港基本法》第 80 條賦予它們的獨立司法權時，有義務執行和解釋《香港基本法》，並審查立法機關和行政機關制定的法律是否符合《香港基本法》，如發現不一致，則裁定無效。[2]

第三，從歷史上看，英方主動建議香港特區法院在 1997 年以後繼續行使違"憲"審查權，中方同意了。這一點是來自參加中英香港問題談判的中國高級官員在回憶錄中的記載。1988 年 2 月，英方提出設立香港特區終審法院的建議大綱，旨在通過在香港特別行政區成立前設立終審法院，提前實現香港的終審權力的配置。本著友好合作的精神，中方對此認真研究了半年，認為早期的過渡性安排將有助於增強香港人民的信心，並決定與英國進行磋商。經過多次協商，英方於 1995 年 5 月 31 日提出了五項

1　胡錦光：《論香港基本法審查權及其界限》，載《武漢大學學報》2017 年第 6 期，第 62 頁。

2　*Leung Kwok Hung v. Secretary for Justice and CEIC*, CACV 541, 542 & 583/2019, para. 64.

意見，其中包括希望中國承認英方在違"憲"審查權和判決救濟機制上的立場。關於英方的新計畫，中方談判小組立即向高層報告。1995 年 6 月 1 日上午，北京及時答覆，均同意英國方提出的五點意見。1995 年 6 月 9 日，中英簽署了正式協定。這確保香港特區法院的違"憲"審查權在 1997 年回歸後繼續行使。[1]

自回歸以來，香港特區法院多次行使違"憲"審查權，一度使香港特區政府與香港特區法院之間的關係陷入前所未有的緊張狀態。香港學者指出，香港在回歸之前雖然有一個最高法院，但最高法院沒有終審權。當事人如果不服最高法院的裁判，可以上訴到在倫敦的樞密院司法委員會。回歸前香港的法院不需要處理涉及"憲法"的案件，香港的法官並沒有處理"憲法"案件的實踐經驗和要求。在英國的普通法體系中，並沒有對違"憲"審查的程序或操作作出規定。在此情況下，法官扮演的角色和承擔的功能是純粹的、專業的和機械的。他們只需根據法律和事實來審理案件，不用考慮亦不受其他任何因素的影響，特別是左右他們判斷的個人的價值取向或個人對某人或某事的看法，更是不受其影響。在此情況下，法官只是法律

1　陳佐洱：《設立香港特區終審法院的中英談判》，載《縱橫》2012 年第 8 期，第 45-46 頁。

工具而已。在英國這種司法制度中，法官不需要對個人權利和社會利益之間的衝突進行平衡，亦不需要在不同的法律價值衝突中作選擇。上述這些問題都是由人民的政治代表在立法過程中考慮的，這些政治決定是由立法機關作出的。[1]而回歸後，《香港基本法》是一部憲制性法律。在解釋"憲法"時，香港特區法院的法官仍舊不採用解釋一般法律的方法，而只從字面意思來解釋它的意思。對"憲法"的解釋涉及到社會價值觀、公共利益和私人利益與權力之間的平衡，這是一種非常政治化的行為。[2]雖然政治問題的司法化已成為民主憲政制度中的一種普遍現象，但是香港特區的法官並不能完全勝任這項艱巨的任務。這次，香港特區高等法院原訟庭對《緊急條例》的判決再次證實了上述觀點。

總之，香港特別行政區法院要尊重全國人民代表大會常務委員會的權威，對於全國人民代表大會常務委員會宣佈合乎《香港基本法》的法律，不能宣佈其違反《香港基本法》。但我們不能因此否定香港特區法院對於立法會立法中僅涉及自治事項條款的審查權，"特區法院的司法

1　邵善波：《成文憲法對香港原有司法體制的影響》，載《港澳研究》2007年冬季號，第67頁。

2　同上，第76頁。

實踐表明違基審查權總體上對基本法實施是有利的"[1]。香港特區法院對於立法會立法中僅涉及自治事項條款的審查權，不僅是實施"一國兩制"的需要，亦是落實《香港基本法》所建構起的法治秩序的需要。

1　李樹忠、姚國建：《香港特區法院的違基審查權 —— 兼與董立坤、張淑鈿二位教授商榷》，載《法學研究》2012 年第 2 期，第 43 頁。

第五章

香港特區《緊急條例》的缺陷

——與英國《國民緊急應變法（2004）》比較

雖然《緊急條例》符合《香港基本法》，但因其是一百年前制定的，自身難免存在缺陷。鑒於香港特區與英國都屬於普通法地區，而且英國的《國民緊急應變法（2004）》較為完善，故以英國的《國民緊急應變法（2004）》為比較對象，來查找香港《緊急條例》的不足。通過與英國《國民緊急應變法（2004）》在文本結構、"緊急狀態"定義、緊急權行使程序、權利保護和權力制約等方面的比較，很容易發現《緊急條例》存在眾多明顯缺陷。

第一節　文本結構的比較

香港《緊急條例》與英國《國民緊急應變法（2004）》的文本之間最直觀的不同是條文數量相差懸殊。英國《國民緊急應變法（2004）》包括正文和三個規劃，正文共 36 條，三個規劃合計 64 條以及 1 份清單，而香港《緊急條例》的條文僅有 4 條。英國《國民緊急應變法（2004）》對一些具體概念、原則、程序等的闡述非常細緻，相比之下，香港《緊急條例》的文本內容則顯得非常簡單粗陋。

除了條文數量的差異外，文本結構邏輯方面兩者亦存在較大差異。英國《國民緊急應變法（2004）》分三部分：第一部分是民防保護的地方安排，第二部分是緊急事件權力，第三部分是概要。按照先概念後程序的邏輯排列，每一部分又分別按照一定的邏輯思路列出對應的內容。比如第一部分"民防保護的地方安排"就分別列出了引言、緊急事件計畫、民防保護、常規等四個部分，按照緊急狀態的內涵外延，分門別類，層層遞進列舉。再如，第二部分"緊急事件權力"，從緊急時刻的定義開始，接著規定制定緊急事件條例的權力主體、範圍、條件、限度、協調和議會的程序，整個過程清晰完整，邏輯嚴謹。反觀香港特區《緊急條例》的文本，只有第 2、3 條涉及主要內容，其中第 2 條列舉了訂立規例的原則，第 3 條列舉了罰則，內容都籠統簡單，缺乏層次和邏輯，立法思路不嚴謹，條文結構不完整。

兩種法律文本在條文數量和文本邏輯架構上形成如此強烈的反差，可以看出立法者對緊急法的立法目的、功能和定位以及對緊急立法的理論認識存在巨大差異，亦預示了兩者在現實中的實施效果將會大有不同。

第二節 "緊急狀態" 定義的比較

何謂 "緊急狀態"？對此問題的回答將決定緊急權啟動的原因和適用的範圍，對緊急立法權的行使有決定性作用。緊急狀態是一種持續或迫在眉睫的危險局勢，不但會危及一個國家的正常的憲政秩序和法律秩序，還會對一國人民的生命和財產安全造成嚴重威脅。[1]事實上，不同國家的立法對緊急狀態有不同的名稱，如 "緊急狀態"、"戒嚴"、"戰爭" 等。[2]每一個名稱都與一國的歷史、國情、文化、傳統、法律制度等緊密相關。儘管描述不盡相同，但大致的內容是相似的。不同的是對緊急狀態內涵和外延的解釋，特別是對緊急權要素規定的不同，有些規定得很詳細，有些則簡略。綜合對緊急狀態的各種定義，根據緊急程度的不同，基本可以劃分為兩類：一類是涉及國家主權安全的，另一類是涉及社會秩序安全的。這樣區分的目的是要明確不同緊急程度對權利克減的程度不同，緊急權

1 莫紀宏：《緊急狀態入憲的意義》，載《法學家》2004 年第 4 期，第 17 頁。
2 李潤田：《各國如何應對緊急態》，http://www.people.com.cn/GB/junshi/1078/2948705.html?5ovxi（最後登錄日期：2020 年 12 月 2 日）。

運行的模式亦不同。兩類緊急狀態不是截然分開，而是在一定條件下可以相互影響和轉化。

英國《國民緊急應變法（2004）》第 1 條規定，緊急是指在英國境內發生的具有嚴重威脅的或損害了人民的利益、環境和英國安全的事件或狀態。其中，涉及威脅、損害人民利益的事件或狀態包括：生命損失、民眾生病或受傷、無家可歸、財產損失、資金、食物、水、能源或燃料供給中斷、通訊系統中斷、運輸設備中斷或者與醫療衛生相關的服務中斷。而涉及威脅損害環境的事件或狀態包括：土地、水或空氣受到生物、化學或核輻射的污染、植物或動物毀滅。該法第 1 條還對緊急狀態的認定作了認定主體和認定細節上的補充。總之，英國《國民緊急應變法（2004）》對緊急權的內涵和外延作了明確的定義，對緊急權的權力主體、權力客體、權力目的、權力手段、權力結果等要素都有詳細的界定，對緊急權的範圍、行使方式和可預見的後果有清晰的規定，使英國緊急權的行使有章可循，減少了行使的阻礙，亦強化了行使的效力。

香港特區《緊急條例》提出了"緊急情況"和"危害公安"的概念，但並沒有對其內涵和外延進行必要的解釋。《緊急條例》涉及的"緊急情況"和"危害公安"屬於香港特別行政區高度自治的內容，與《香港基本法》規定的涉及國家主權的緊急狀態有本質的區別，不能將兩者等同。正如上任行政長官林鄭月娥所說，《緊急條例》中的"緊急情況"和"危害公安"並非《香港基本法》的"緊急狀態"。[1] 從字面上看，《緊急條例》和《香港基本法》對"緊急"的表述不同，《緊急條例》使用"緊急情況"一詞，而《香港基本法》則使用"緊急狀態"一詞。對關鍵概念缺乏必要、完整的定義，勢必會讓人對緊急權在何種情況下能夠啟動以及如何確保緊急權合法行使產生質疑。

---

1 《港府引用"緊急法"開先例，外界憂隨時"加辣"》，https://www.rfa.org/cantonese/news/htm/hk-emergency-10042019094047.html（最後登錄日期：2019 年 12 月 10 日）。

第三節　緊急權行使程序的比較

　　對緊急狀態概念的內涵、外延、要素、種類的認定屬於緊急權的實體要件。實體要件對緊急權存在的正當性、合法性有決定作用，但僅有實體要件還不足以保證緊急權實施的正當合法，必須有一套合理、完整的程序要件來確保緊急權得以正當和合法實施。鑒於緊急權具有許可權大、容易失控或造成對基本權利侵害的特點，參考部分學者的研究成果和對各國已有緊急法內容的總結，可將緊急權行使的基本程序歸納為以下七個步驟：緊急情況或緊急狀態的預防、確認、宣佈、期限、終止、監督和事後對秩序的恢復。[1]

　　英國《國民緊急應變法（2004）》的內容雖然沒有與上述的七個步驟一一對應列明，但其全文基本涵蓋了七個步驟。在第一部分"民防保護的地方安排"的"緊急事件計畫"部分第 2 條"評估、計畫或建議的職責"裏面，對緊急狀態的預防作了詳細的規定；第一部分"民防保護的

1　戚建剛：《中國行政應急法律制度研究》，北京：北京大學出版社 2010 年版，第 95-125 頁。

地方安排"第 1 條"緊急事件的定義"和第二部分"緊急事件權力"第 19 條"緊急時刻的定義"，對緊急狀態的概念和確認作了明確的規定；第一部分"民防保護的地方安排"第 6 條"資訊的發佈"，對緊急權相關資訊的宣佈作了規定；第二部分"緊急事件權力"第 26 條"持續時間"，對期限和終止作了明確規定；對緊急情況的處理、監督方面則貫穿整個緊急法文本。此外，第一部分"民防保護的地方安排"的"民防保護"部分第 5 條"總體措施"、第一部分"民防保護的地方安排"的"常規"部分對緊急權的執行，包括在蘇格蘭、威爾士的執行，都進行了詳細的規定；第二部分"緊急事件權力"第 20 至 31 條，對"制定緊急事件條例的權力"進行了非常詳盡的規定，包括制定緊急事件條例的權力主體、條件、範圍、限度、協調者、期限、程序、特別法庭的建立、議會詳細審查（包括休會和延期的操作）、移交管理部門的協商和解釋等。

香港特區《緊急條例》賦予行政長官的緊急立法權無論是實體要件，還是程序要件在詳細程度上都難以與英國《國民緊急應變法（2004）》相提並論。《緊急條例》只賦予了行政長官立法的權力，對其立法的範圍和罰則作了簡單的規定，沒有列明具體的立法條件和程序，特別是對期限、立法會審查、相關部門協商等環節缺少設計，容易造成緊急立法權被濫用，很可能會對基本權利造成侵害，這就難免讓人對緊急權產生擔憂。如果說對緊急權本質和原理的理解疏漏是香港《緊急條例》遭到質疑的根本原因，那麼緊急權程序要件上的缺失則是其遭到質疑的直接原因。

第四節　權利保護的比較

美國經濟學家亞瑟·奧肯認為：“有時會為了效率而犧牲一些公平，有時又會為了公平而犧牲一些效率。但任何一種犧牲，都必須作為增進另一方的必要手段，否則便沒有理由這麼做。”[1] 美國的路易士·亨金認為：“權利觀念承認對權利的一定限制是允許的，但限制本身應該受到嚴格限制。”[2] 由此可見，緊急權力和其他的國家權力有不同之處。其他國家權力由公民讓渡的權利產生，其目的主要是保障權利的實現；而緊急權則不同，其緊急情況的特性會讓權利和權力的關聯式結構產生改變（主要是權力對權利的限制甚至侵害），沒有這種改變就不會有緊急權的產生。這是緊急權能集中力量應付處理緊急情況的主要原因，亦是緊急權區別於其他權力之處。

緊急狀態下公民權利會被克減，但這種克減的範圍、方式需要遵守一定原則。首先，必須符合必要理論，即具

---

1 （美）亞瑟·奧肯：《平等與效率》，王奔洲譯，北京：華夏出版社 1987 年版，第 105 頁。

2 （美）路易士·亨金：《權利的時代》，信春鷹等譯，北京：知識出版社 1997 年版，第 5 頁。

有正當性、緊迫性。必要理論是最早的非常法律理論，起源於 12 世紀，教會法學家格拉提安（Flavius Gratianus）在其著作《格拉提安教令集》中提出了"必要之事無須法律"的著名法律格言，近代以後化身為戒嚴法的淵源。[1]其次，必須符合權利理論，權利理論是現代法律理論的核心，亦是非常法律的基礎理論。權利理論起源於自然權利理論，作為非常法律理論的基礎理論之一，包含了三個方面：一是個人享有基本權利；二是國家應當承擔相關義務；三是緊急情況下的權利克減應該受到限制。[2]世界各國對緊急狀態下公民權利克減的範圍、程度、方式的規定各不相同，但基本上都參照了《世界人權宣言》、聯合國有關國際人權保護的三個公約[3]關於人權保護的內容和原則。其中，《公民權利和政治權利國際公約》第 4 條第 1 款規定："在社會緊急狀態威脅到國家的生命並經正式宣佈時，本公約締約國得採取措施克減其在本公約下所承擔的義務，但克減的程度以緊急情勢所嚴格需要者為限，此等措施並不得與它根據國際法所負有的其他義務相矛盾，且不得包含純

1　孟濤：《中國非常法律研究》，北京：清華大學出版社 2012 年版，第 201-203 頁。

2　同上，第 203-206 頁。

3　三個公約是指《經濟、社會與文化權利的國際公約》（A 公約）、《公民權利和政治權利國際公約》（B 公約）和《公民權利和政治權利國際公約任擇議定書》（B 公約議定書）。

粹基於種族、膚色、性別、語言、宗教或社會出身的理由的歧視。"第 2 款規定："不得根據本規定而克減第六條、第七條、第八條（第一款和第二款）、第十一條、第十五條、第十六條和第十八條。"第 15 條第 1 款規定："任何人的任何行為或不行為，在其發生時依照國家法或國際法均不構成刑事罪者，不得據以認為犯有刑事罪。所加的刑罰亦不得重於犯罪時適用的規定。如果在犯罪之後依法規定了應處以較輕的刑罰，犯罪者應予減刑。"

英國《國民緊急應變法（2004）》在權利克減的監督和限制上規定得很全面，體現了對《公民權利和政治權利國際公約》權利克減原則的遵守。首先，權利克減是被動的，是在現有立法不足以應付緊急狀況的前提下才能夠進行。這在該法中表現為第 21 條"制定緊急條例的條件"的第 5 款提到"現有立法不能信賴（具有嚴重耽擱的風險）"、第 6 款提到"在現有立法下制定的制度可能無效"。其次，該法在克減的程序方面作了嚴格限制。該法第 19 至 30 條對緊急狀態的定義，對制定緊急事件條例的權力範圍、條件和程序都作了嚴格的界定。再次，該法在克減的程度方面作了嚴格限制。該法第 23 條"緊急事件條例的限度"的第 1 款第 a 項和第 b 項明確規定了"條例的制定適合預防、控制或減緩緊急事件的一個方面或效果，條例的效果與緊急事件的影響方面成正比。"復次，該法對不能克減的權利作出了明確規定。該法第 23 條第 3 款、第 4 款詳細列明所制定的緊急事件條例不可以：(a) 要求一個人，或者使一個人被要求服軍役，或者（b）禁止或使之禁止參與罷工或者任何與罷工相聯繫的其他行為。該條第 5 款規定所制定的緊急事件條例不能修正：(a) 本法案的這個部分，或者（b）1998 年人權法案。最後，該法對違反相關條例的懲罰作出刑罰上的明確規定。該法第 23 條第 4 款第 c 項規定所制定的緊急事件條例不可以創設可處以以下刑罰的罪行：(i) 超過 3 個月的拘禁，或者（ii）超過第五級水準的罰款，第 d 項規定不可以改變與刑事訴訟相關的程序。

香港特區《緊急條例》對權利的克減主要體現在第 2 條第 2 款的規定，但只列明內容，沒有涉及克減的條件、程序和罰則，因而體現不出權利克減應受制約的常理，賦權過於寬泛，以致行政長官引用《緊急條例》制定的《禁止蒙面規例》引發質疑。[1] 香港應該借鑒英國的做法，在權利克減的限制方面作出更合理、更明確的約束。

---

1 《〈禁止蒙面規例〉出臺後，誰慌了？〉》，http://www.bjd.com.cn/a/201910/14/WS5da3c5bee4b0ed1b67c5aba4.html（最後登錄日期：2020 年 4 月 23 日）。

第五節 權力制約的比較

亞里士多德在對法治概念進行闡述時提出了"制定良好的法律"的概念，[1] 後人藉此將法分為善法和惡法，於是緊急權立法相對於其他國家權力在很多時候更容易被定性為惡法。但幾千年來，人們對善惡的求解並沒有一個完美的答案，或許善惡並沒有絕對的界限，不同情境都會給出不同的答案，因此對緊急權和其他國家權力的認識亦應該持對立統一的觀念。

緊急權是在緊急狀態下依法啟動的權力。緊急權的行使很可能會引起原先權力結構的變化，使權力產生交叉或集中，但其本質沒有變化，還是源自基本權利的讓渡。雖然權力的主體、對象、程序、效力產生變化，但目的是為了獲得和維護社會的穩定。緊急權具有集中性，雖然合理合法，但不意味著不受監督和制約。在緊急情況或緊急狀態下，因為權力的集中，緊急權受監督和制約的力度通常要遠遠低於正常狀態下其他國家權力受到的監督和制約力

---

1 （古希臘）亞里士多德：《政治學》，吳壽彭譯，北京：商務印書館 2011 年版，第四卷第八章。

度。對緊急權監督和制約的理想狀態是國家即使在緊急狀態下仍然能堅守必要理論和權利理論，堅持合理和合法的界線，制定詳細可行的自我約束機制。特別是對緊急立法權的監督和制約，要對其效力、時限和審查機制作出必要規定，以最終實現對緊急權的監督和制約。

英國《國民緊急應變法（2004）》第二部分"緊急事件權力"的第 20 條、第 24 至 30 條對"制定緊急事件條例的權力"的條件、範圍、限度和程序作了明確規定，特別規定了協商者、特別法庭和議會審查的程序，體現了對緊急權在立法和司法上的監督和制約。香港特區《緊急條例》在對緊急權的監督和制約方面是缺失的。《緊急條例》在第 2 條第 1、2 款賦予行政長官緊急立法的權力，在第 2 條第 3、4 款從立法的期限和有效性方面繼續強化行政長官的緊急立法權。如果權力只是被賦予而不受監督和制約，就是非常危險的狀態，將導致行政長官緊急立法權被濫用。特別是《緊急條例》第 2 條第 3 款規定，根據本條條文訂立的任何規例，須持續有效至行政長官會同行政會議藉命令廢除為止，這種規定不符合議會具有對行政緊急立法進行"否定性審查"（negative vetting）權力的通常做法。

第六章

香港特區《緊急條例》的完善

因為《緊急條例》存在明顯的缺陷，所以應及時加以完善。完善《緊急條例》的首要工作，是規制香港特區行政長官緊急立法權。鑒於英國的緊急立法比較先進，且香港特區與英國在法制方面有歷史淵源，香港特區《緊急條例》的完善，在具體內容上可以借鑒英國《國民緊急應變法（2004）》。

第一節　香港特區行政長官緊急立法權的規制

　　緊急立法權會克減公民的基本權利，香港特區行政長官的緊急立法權亦不例外，故必須對其加以規制，以防止被濫用。對行政長官緊急立法權的規制應堅持的原則有：必要性原則、比例原則、權利保留原則、資訊公開原則和程序正當原則。對香港特區行政長官的緊急立法權的規制，需要從實體和程序兩個方面展開。

一、規制的未來趨勢

　　緊急立法權是行政機關用以應對緊急狀態的一項重要權力，它是在國家發生緊急狀態而正常的憲法和法律不足以消除危機的情況下，為了維護國家生存並儘快恢復正常秩序，依憲法規定採取的緊急措施。與一般行政權力相比較，緊急立法權具有特殊的特點和功能，即行政機關可以通過行使緊急立法權來制定法律，中止正常狀態下的憲法義務，克減憲法規定的公民基本權利，體現了行政權力的集中和擴張，如果不加以監督制約，很容易被濫用。儘管學術界對緊急立法權的合法性和正當性認識並不一致，但對緊急立法權在應對危機時具有重大作用的觀點已達成共識。同時，學術界亦對緊急立法權的缺點存在共同隱憂，緊急立法權因為具有限制正常狀態下不能限制的公民權利的權能，所以會被詬病具有對憲政原則的違背和對公民基本權利的侵害的缺點。綜上所述，緊急立法權作為行政緊急權的體現，應該與其他緊急權力一樣，自產生之初就受到監督和制約。對行政緊急權的規制歷史悠久，在人權發展史上最早的幾部重要法典裏，都體現了對行政緊急權的監督和制約。目前，許多國家的憲法條文都設有"緊急狀態條款"（或稱"緊急權條款"）。因此，中國內地學者王禎軍認為規制行政緊急權具有以下三點重要的意義：一是為行政緊急權的行使提供正當性；二是確保行政緊急權在法治框架內行使；三是加強對公民基本權利的保護。另外，王禎軍還提出了規制行政緊急權的主要模式：一是授予行政緊急權；二是限制行政緊急權。[1]

綜上所述，緊急立法權的規制跟行政緊急權的規制密不可分，基本上遵循了行政緊急權規制的方向、模式和原則，從對行政緊急權規制的內容亦可以得出對緊急立法權規制的內容。儘管目前各國規制緊急立法權的模式存在差異，但基本都是採用憲法或專門的緊急法對其進行直接規

---

[1] 王禎軍：《論行政緊急權的憲法規制》，載《河北法學》2017 年第 7 期，第 53-54 頁。

定的模式。在授予行政機關緊急立法權的同時，需要對緊急立法權的行使進行制約。這亦是規制香港特區行政長官緊急立法權的未來趨勢，即用法治理念和制定更細化的法律文件來規制緊急立法權。

二、規制的基本原則

從法理學的角度來看，法律原則比法律規則更能體現法律的基本價值，在缺乏具體的緊急立法權實施細則的情況下，法律原則可作為緊急立法權行使的指引。另外，由於法律原則比法律規則具有更大的彈性，緊急立法權規制模式的設計既要充分發揮緊急立法權在應對危機方面的高效性，又要防止緊急立法權被濫用的危險。由此可見，運用法律原則是一種比較合適的規制手段。

世界各國對緊急立法權的規制主要遵循了對國家緊急權規制的原則，而對國家緊急權規制原則設置的依據主要源於《公民權利和政治權利國際公約》第 4 條[1]的內容。

---

1 《公民權利和政治權利國際公約》第 4 條規定：一、在社會緊急狀態威脅到國家的生命並經正式宣佈時，本公約締約國得採取措施克減其在本公約下所承擔的義務，但克減的程度以緊急情勢所嚴格需要者為限，此等措施並不得與它根據國際法所負有的其他義務相矛盾，且不得包含純粹基於種族、膚色、性別、語言、宗教或社會出身的理由的歧視。二、不得根據本規定而克減第 6 條、第 7 條、第 8 條（第 1 款和第 2 款）、第 11 條、第 15 條、第 16 條和第 18 條。三、任何援用克減權的本公約締約國應立即經由聯合國秘書長將它已克減的各項規定、實行克減的理由和終止這種克減的日期通知本公約的其他締約國家。

該條文設置了國家緊急權行使的原則，主要包括對國家緊急權的監督和對公民權利的保護。具體原則如下：一是必要性原則；二是比例原則；三是權利保留，四是資訊公開原則。各國因為具體情況不一，對國家緊急權規制原則的內容亦有所不同，但基本上都是圍繞對克減公民權利的法律制約這個中心來設置的。

綜上所述，緊急立法權的規制原則可以根據國家緊急權規制的原則進行提煉，主要內容分為實體方面的權力制約和權利保護，以及程序方面的程序正當、資訊公開、司法救濟，具體原則有：必要性原則、比例原則、權利保留原則、資訊公開原則、程序正當原則。對香港特區行政長官緊急立法權的規制同樣可以參照上述的原則進行設置，在具體的操作過程中，可能要考慮到其普通法的傳統以及"一國兩制"的實際情況，才能制定出更加貼合實際而又具有指導意義的原則。

三、規制的基本思路

由於緊急立法權屬於國家緊急權的一部分，對其進行規制必須在國家緊急權法律制度的框架下進行，所以在對緊急立法權進行規制的思路設計上，既要考慮當前完善國家緊急法律制度的需要，亦要著眼於國家未來履行國際人權公約的需要；既要合理借鑒各國法律文本在規制緊急立法權的合理措施，又要充分考慮國家法治和民主建設的實際情況。筆者認為可以按以下操作思路對緊急立法權進行規則。

一、明確緊急立法權規制的原則。通過憲制性文本專門規定一條"緊急狀態條款"，將緊急權規制中涉及到的原則性的問題確定下來，為之後緊急立法權規制提供依據。

二、明確緊急立法權規制的重點內容。對緊急立法權規制的內容可以分為實體和程序兩個方面。由於各國對緊急法的重視，基本上都制定了緊急法律，只是在法律層級上有所不同，但大致上都存在重實體輕程序的問題，即對緊急法的內容規定比較全面，但缺乏可操作性的措施，使得緊急法在應急時變成一紙空文。鑒於此，各國對緊急立法權的規制就更顯得捉襟見肘。

三、明確緊急立法權規制的具體內容。未來對緊急立法權的規制必須做好以下方面：一是明確緊急立法權的授權；二是明確緊急立法權的啟動條件；三是明確緊急立法權宣佈的程序；四是明確緊急立法權的行使程序；五是明確緊急立法權的期限和延長規則；六是明確緊急立法權遵循的法律原則。

作為香港特區行政長官緊急立法權最主要的法律依據，《緊急條例》存在諸多問題，導致香港特區行政長官緊急立法權在行使時受到詬病和挑戰。鑒於此，有必要根據以上規制思路，從實體和程序兩個方面對其進行規制，使其既能在特殊狀況下發揮維護社會穩定的作用，又能避免給居民權利和自由帶來不必要的損害。

第二節 對英國《國民緊急應變法（2004）》的借鑒

香港的《緊急條例》是在一百年前制定的，條文的簡陋導致其正當性遭受質疑，確實有必要進行修改、完善。英國的緊急立法比較先進，且香港特區與英國在法制方面有歷史淵源，香港緊急法的完善可以借鑒英國的做法。借鑒英國《國民緊急應變法（2004）》來完善香港特區《緊急條例》，應列明緊急法對相對人權利保障的具體可行措施，規範以行政長官為主導的緊急權，以及完善《緊急條例》的文本。

一、為何借鑒英國《國民緊急應變法（2004）》？

如前所述，與英國《國民緊急應變法（2004）》相比，在文本結構方面，香港特區《緊急條例》不僅條文數量很少，而且文本內容顯得非常簡單粗陋；在對關鍵概念的定義方面，香港《緊急條例》並沒有對"緊急情況"和"危害公安"的內涵和外延進行必要的解釋；在緊急權行使程序方面，《緊急條例》沒有列明行政長官行使緊急立法權的具體條件和程序，特別是對期限、立法會審查、相關部門協商等環節缺少設計；在權利限制方面，香港特區《緊急條例》對權利克減只列明克減的內容，沒有涉及克減的條件、程序和罰則，體現不出權利克減應受制約的常理；在權力制約方面，香港特區《緊急條例》對如何監督行政長官的緊急立法權缺乏必要的制度安排。由以上可見，香港特區《緊急條例》確實具有修改、完善的必要性。

香港特區《緊急條例》條文的簡陋導致其正當性遭受質疑，由此引發行政長官能否擁有緊急立法權的訴訟。香港特區行政長官會同行政會議依據《緊急條例》訂定《禁止蒙面規例》，不但沒有發揮應有的治亂止暴的作用，而且引致更多對政府治理行為合憲性的質疑。香港特區《緊急條例》面臨挑戰的一個重要原因是對緊急權失控的擔憂。

英國在民防立法方面頗有經驗。英國早在 1920 年就制定了《緊急權力法》（*Emergency Powers Act*）。但真正作為英國應急管理基礎的是 1948 年的《民防法》（*The Civil Denfence Act*），該法對當時防禦戰爭引致的危害起到了積極作用。《國民緊急應變法（2004）》是在 1948 年《民防法》基礎上，因應新形勢而制定，所涉及的內容比較全面。英國內閣辦公室還依據《國民緊急應變法（2004）》於 2013 年 10 月 29 日提出 "緊急應變與復原準則：依循 2004 年國民緊急應變法之不成文準則"
（Emergency Response and Recovery: Non Statutory Guidance
Accompanying *the Civil Contingencies Act 2004*），針對
"應變與復原"作出相關規定。此規則於"緊急應變章
節"規定地方政府之緊急事件依嚴重程度區分為三級：
銅（Bronze），即僅需要操作指揮（Operational）；銀
（Silver），即需要策略指揮（Tactical）；和金（Gold），即
需要戰略指揮（Strategic），以此來判斷是否需要跨機關
合作來應對緊急事故。如果事故屬於重大緊急災難時，就
屬於需要跨機關協調合作，此時須藉由層級指揮及指令
下達來掌控應變程序與資訊傳遞，以因應長期及廣泛區
域的災難。中央政府的權責在於處理全國性重大緊急事
件，並且災難發生時的首相為最高行政首長，最高緊急機
構為"內閣緊急應變會議"（Cabinet Office Brifing Rooms,
COBR，又稱為眼鏡蛇），同時國民緊急秘書處（Civil
Contingencies Secretariat, CCS）亦需要協調跨部門及跨機
構的事務。[1]總之，英國的緊急立法比較先進，而由於香港
與英國在法制方面有歷史淵源，香港在緊急法上的完善可

---

[1] 《英國提出"緊急應變與復原準則"強化災難時之應變規定》，https://stli.
iii.org.tw/article-detail.aspx?no=64&tp=1&d=6528（最後登錄日期：2022 年
12 月 1 日）。

以借鑒英國的做法。當然，香港畢竟已經回歸中國，並成為中國主權下的一個特別行政區，這決定了香港的緊急立法不能生搬硬套英國的模式，而必須充分考慮香港的實際情況，認清香港在國家體系中所處的地位和目前香港緊急情況的地方層級屬性。故此，香港特區《緊急條例》的修改和完善必須符合"一國兩制"和《香港基本法》等憲制文件的規定。

二、如何借鑒英國《國民緊急應變法（2004）》？

（一）列明緊急法對於相對人權利保障的具體可行措施

人們對緊急權的態度歷來存在輕視或恐懼兩種傾向。輕視是認為和平年代下不太可能發生緊急狀況，故對緊急權下自身權利的變化沒有具體的認知。恐懼則是因為自古以來戰火紛飛、國破家亡和王朝更迭大多是由於緊急權的行使，即集權和專制盛行使得民眾權利遭受巨大侵害。無論輕視或是恐懼，圍繞的一個核心思想是緊急權下如何對權利進行保障。正如馬基雅維利所說："危急時期的共和國，如果在大災難臨頭之際，不要求於專政，往往會走上覆滅"，而盧梭亦曾說："人民的首要意願是：國家不應滅亡。"[1] 因此，有國家就會有緊急權，任何試圖擺脫緊急權的企圖都是一種幻想，迄今為止人類的發展歷史印證了這一點。我們只能通過制度和法律的設計，讓緊急權不至於脫離賦權者的控制。

通過前文對緊急權的闡述，我們可知，由於緊急權的集權性很容易對相對人的權利造成限制甚至傷害，所以緊急權下如何保障相對人的權利的很重要的一環就是對緊急權的限制。實現對緊急權的限制有兩方面的要求：一方面，權利克減本質上不可能是權利保障，故緊急法如果是以權利保障為指導思想，那麼其規定的權利克減在限制權利上必須是消極的、被動的。另一方面，在法律文本上明示權利克減受到監督，最大限度保障相對人的權利。比較上述兩個方面，對於建立或完善一部緊急法而言，列明緊急法對相對人權利保障的具體可行措施更為切實有效。

如何做好在緊急法中列明對相對人權利保障的具體可行措施呢？人們藉助自身智慧和政治經驗，完全有可能通過對制度和法律的設計，讓緊急權不至於脫離賦權者的控制，亦有條件、有能力在緊急權未被使用之前就為之設置好基本原則和制度。因此，一部體現權利保障思想的緊急

---

1 （美）羅斯托：《憲法專政：現代民主國家種中的危機政府》，孟濤譯，北京：華夏出版社 2015 年版，扉頁。

法必定會在條文中詳細列明保障相對人權利的基本原則和措施，明確列明權利克減的條件、程度和救濟等。這樣，在緊急狀況發生之際，我們才能對權利克減的威脅程度有一個基本的預測。另外，緊急法還必須設置相關的監督機構，制定相關的追責條款，在緊急權遭到濫用、權利克減失衡的時候，可以有效制止濫用者的行為，追究濫用者的責任。只有這樣，才能使緊急權行使和權利克減都在預設的框架內實施，使國家、公民的福祉和緊急權的行使達成一個相對平衡的狀態，最大限度維護公民的各項基本權利。

在緊急法列明相對人權利保障措施方面，英國《國民緊急應變法（2004）》做得非常到位。如前文所述，其法律文本的第 19-30 條裏面詳細列明了英國在緊急狀態下權利克減的適用條件、克減程度、克減程序、對克減的限制和克減可能產生的責任。香港特區《緊急條例》在第 2 條共 14 款中對緊急狀態下的權利克減亦作了規定，說明香港《緊急條例》具有保障相對人權利的思想，但另一方面，條例只有粗略的內容，不具備可操作性，沒有很好體現對權利克減的限制，說明《緊急條例》保障相對人權利的具體措施不到位。但這並不意味著香港特區在權利保障意識方面的淡薄。相反，從前文所述香港特區高等法院的審理過程可以看出，特區政府、法院、申請人的權利保障意識還是很強的。香港社會對《緊急條例》不滿的原因除了擔憂政府在行使緊急權時不能嚴格遵守有關原則外，更直接的原因是不滿《緊急條例》對相對人權利保障方面缺乏具體可行的措施。因此，完善香港特區《緊急條例》可以借鑒英國的做法，在保障相對人權利思想的指引下，結合香港的實際，對緊急權下的權利克減作出詳細、可操作的規定，並在條例中明示出來。

（二）規範以行政長官為主導的緊急權

回顧歷史，香港在經濟和社會管理方面取得成功，行政主導的治理模式功不可沒，而行政主導的順利實施需要豐富的行政法律法規支持。香港的行政法的重要特點之一是其包括了許多部門和不同層級的行政法規範，這些條例、規例、附則、規則和法令等涉及社會和經濟管理的各個方面，構成香港行政法的淵源。雖然香港行政法的形式和層次多元且內容豐富，但是行政立法並不因此而喪失嚴肅性和周密性。例如，在制定行政條例的程序方面，幾乎所有涉及到的香港特區政府機構及非官方機構都設有諮詢組織以收集各方意見，為政府的立法和決策提供參考。另外，行政條例草案擬好以後須經行政、立法兩局議員進行審議才能正式提交立法局公開辯論，最後在立法局上三讀通過才能實施，從而保證行政立法的穩定性。香港行政法的另一個重要特點是行政主導模式的受制約性，它要求政府嚴格執法，並建立香港的司法審查和行政訴訟制度。[1]

目前香港特區實施"一國兩制"，香港的政治體制是行政長官負責制下的行政主導模式，充分體現了香港社會行政法治的傳統和特點。行政長官對中央人民政府負責，對香港特區負責，其有天然的優勢在緊急情況下作為行使緊急權的主體。當緊急情況發生時，需要高度集權才能調動各方資源應急處理，香港特區的行政、立法、司法三機關中只有行政機關才能勝任對緊急情況進行及時、高效的處理。另外，香港特區《緊急條例》亦規定了行政長官在緊急情況下可以會同行政會議行使緊急權，這就是以法律的形式確認以行政長官為主導的緊急權模式。然而，行政長官主導的緊急權模式不是指行政長官或特區政府擁有無限的緊急權，而應該是一種可以預見的權力的行使。因為行政長官及其領導的特區政府為了有效應對緊急情況，一般通過採取各類手段和措施，其中包括制定和發佈應急法律規範，這些法律規範可能會涉及強制措施、徵用，甚至剝奪人身自由的刑罰（包括終身監禁）。唯有將政府緊急

1　楊海坤：《對香港行政法的觀察與思考》，載《行政法學研究》1996 年第 1 期，第 29-33 頁。

權的邊界和責任設定下來，才能確保緊急權只用來恢復正常秩序，從而避免淪為專制的藉口和工具。一百年前，港英政府頒佈《緊急條例》是為了鎮壓參加香港海員大罷工的華人，其規定港督會同行政局訂立的緊急法可以設置終身監禁的刑罰，是極其嚴酷的，在世界上也極為罕見。《緊急條例》頒佈一百年後的今天，如果仍然堅持此嚴刑酷法，就嚴重不符合現代文明社會的罪刑相適應的原則。因此，規範以行政長官為主導的緊急權，非常重要的一項內容是嚴格控制行政長官會同行政會議訂立附屬法規所設立的剝奪人身自由的刑罰。具體可參考英國的有關做法，把剝奪人身自由的刑罰限定為最長五年。

香港特區《緊急條例》的文本粗陋，難以體現香港行政立法的嚴肅性和周密性，使得行政主導模式的受制約性遭到質疑，沒能充分發揮香港特區行政長官為主導的緊急權模式的優勢。為了避免緊急權特別是行政長官的緊急立法權被濫用，緊急權的行使除了堅持正當性和合法性的原則外，在具體運作上可以部分借鑒英國的做法，使緊急權的立法受到立法會的制約。《國民緊急應變法（2004）》第 26 條規定了英國行政機關制定的緊急條例有效期只有三十天，可以提前失效，亦可以在三十天後制定新的緊急法律。在第 27 條第 1 款第 a 項中規定一旦緊急條例被制定出來，必須由一名高級內閣大臣儘快以合理可行的方式將緊急條例遞交給議會兩院審查批准。此外，在第 27 條第 4 款中規定"在本節中沒有任何東西能夠阻止制定新的條例，或者將不會影響緊急條例失效、終止生效或被修正之前所做的任何事。"以上條文充分說明英國在緊急立法權方面，行政機關和立法機關既相互獨立又相互制約。鑒於香港特區行政、立法、司法三權配置的模式與英國議會至上的模式不同，香港特區《緊急條例》的完善，除了要發揮香港特區行政主導和行政法治的傳統和優勢外，還應該學習英國對緊急立法權的制約意識，處理好香港特區的行政、立法和司法三者的關係，特別是行政機關的緊急立法應該先由行政機關訂立後由立法機關審議，而且司法機關對行政機關的緊急立法有審查的權力，從而確保緊急權不被濫用，更好地完善以行政長官為主導的緊急權模式。

關於特區立法會對行政長官會同行政會議制定的緊急法的監督問題，香港特區高等法院原訟庭指出，儘管《緊急條例》賦予行政長官會同行政會議制定規例的權力，但立法會仍保留對任何規例進行否定性審查的角色，權力依據是《釋義及通則條例》第 34 條。[1] 雖然《緊急條例》第 2

---

[1] *Leung Kwok Hung v. Secretary for Justice and CEIC*, HCAL 2945/2019, para. 69.

條第 3 款規定，根據本條文訂立的任何規例，須持續有效至行政長官會同行政會議藉命令廢除為止，但該條款本身並不妨礙立法會根據《釋義及通則條例》第 34 條的規定廢除該等規例，或該規例被其後的條例廢除。[1] 香港特區高等法院上訴庭認同原訟庭的以上觀點，並指出特區立法會對依據《緊急條例》所制定的規例具有有效性和效力的時限，亦有持續審查的機制。因為根據《釋義及通則條例》第 34 條規定的否定性審查程序，首先存在第一階段的審查，即在二十八天的期限屆滿之前，條例生效，該期限可以延長二十一天。如果條例在否定性審查期間被廢除，則該規定的有效期將不會超過該期限。此外，即使條例經否定性審查後繼續生效，立法會亦會透過第二階段的審查，進一步檢討有關條例。[2] 香港特區終審法院亦認為，《釋義及通則條例》的第 34 條規定特區立法會可對根據《緊急條例》制定的任何法規進行否決性審查，這些文件須在規例刊登憲報後的立法會下次會議上提交立法會省覽。[3] 筆者認為，因為《緊急條例》第 2 條第 3 款的上述規定是

1　Ibid, para. 72.

2　*Leung Kwok Hung v. Secretary for Justice and CEIC*, CACV 541/2019, para. 150.

3　*Leung Kwok Hung v. Secretary for Justice and CEIC*, FACV nos. 6, 7, 8 and 9 of 2020, [2020] HKCFA 42, para. 57.

1997 年修訂的結果，而《釋義及通則條例》的第 34 條在此之前就存在，故立法會不可依據《釋義及通則條例》的第 34 條對依據《緊急條例》制定的條例進行否定性審查。但議會對包括政府緊急立法在內的附屬立法進行審查是英國的通常做法，香港特區立法會亦應有權否定行政長官會同行政會議訂立的緊急立法。綜合以上，《緊急條例》中的"根據本條例制定的任何條例應繼續有效、直至行政長官會同行政會議下令廢除"的規定，應刪去，以消除特區立法會對行政長官緊急立法進行監督的障礙。

（三）完善香港《緊急條例》的文本

完善《緊急條例》的文本，需要從兩個方面著手：一方面是重構《緊急條例》框架；另一方面是細化文本的內容。

就重構《緊急條例》的框架而言，立法者要明確"緊急情況"和"危害公安"的內涵和外延，明確香港《緊急條例》主要是適用於社會動亂，強調政府的緊急權更多屬於社會緊急事件的應急處理，以區別於國家層面的緊急狀態。《緊急條例》對緊急情況的定義、範圍、條件、決定機關、宣佈機關、程序等應有具體規定，明確建立以行政長官為主導的緊急權模式；列明行政、立法、司法三個機關之間的協調和制約關係；明確對權利克減的規定和限制，完善對基本權利的立法保護和司法救濟。對行政長官主導的緊急權模式的規範，除了考慮立法機關、司法機關的作用外，還應考慮中央政府的作用。香港畢竟是中央政府直轄下的特別行政區，不同於國家或獨立政治實體，對行政長官權力的監控，不能忽略中央政府的作用，尤其是在涉及對居民權利克減這種重大事宜上。因香港特區行政長官會同行政會議訂立的緊急立法不用報全國人民代表大會常務委員會備案，中央政府對此緊急立法的監控可以體現為行政長官事先向中央政府的彙報、諮詢，這些內容可以寫入《緊急條例》。

就細化文本的內容而言，立法技術一般服務於立法目的，有些法律採取概括的立法方式，是因為所涉法律情況不可預知，故在條文中作留白或概括處理。但是緊急權、特別是緊急立法權的行使容易造成權力濫用，為了避免任何法外之法或是自行變通，緊急法的制定不宜採取概括式立法，而應該詳細和謹慎地構建整個法律架構和內容。香港特區《緊急條例》只有四條，之前的立法者應該不只是出於概括式立法容易變通的考慮，更多的是出於英國為了維護自己利益和實現港督治港，而對港督進行的廣泛授權而為之。香港可以借鑒英國《國民緊急應變法（2004）》的文本，在文本的結構邏輯和內容上取其精華，細化緊急權的範圍以及行使的程序，讓香港特區《緊急條例》更具正當性和操作性。細化香港特區《緊急條例》文本的一項非常重要的工作是對其中的"緊急情況"進行定義。然而，香港特區高等法院上訴庭認為，就性質而言，"緊急情況"或"危害公安"不可能有詳盡的定義，可能提供的任何定義都必須是籠統或寬泛的。[1]筆者對此不敢苟同，認為還是應儘可能對這種關鍵概念進行定義。鑒於《公安條例》中"危害公安"的行為內涵廣泛，包括非法集結、非法遊行、炸彈嚇詐、暴動等，而非法集結、非法遊行等一般違法犯罪行為不宜作為制定緊急法的理由，即應對這種情況不需要制定緊急法，故建議把"危害公安"中的暴動納入"緊急情況"，然後把"危害公安"從《緊急條例》中刪去，不作為緊急立法的事由和依據。此做法既能與國際通行做法接軌，又能最大化避免引致爭議。

1　*Leung Kwok Hung v. Secretary for Justice and CEIC*, CACV 541/2019, para. 126.

結語

2019 年 10 月，時任香港特區行政長官林鄭月娥會同行政會議作出決定，根據《緊急條例》訂立《禁止蒙面規例》，是為了儘快平息暴亂，恢復法治秩序，但該規例的頒佈又引致一些爭議和訴訟。行政緊急權是緊急狀態下最重要的一種公權力，突發事件的突然性、緊迫性、嚴重性決定了只有行政機關才能勝任緊急立法此種職責。雖然《香港基本法》沒有為香港特區政府就維護香港本地的安全而設置相應的緊急情況處置權，但是由於香港特區政府對該地區的法律和秩序負有主要責任，它應該擁有一些緊急權。況且這種緊急權亦得到作為構建香港憲制不可或缺的《香港人權法案條例》的確認。

　　香港特區高等法院上訴庭和終審法院裁判行政長官會同行政會議依據《緊急條例》訂定《禁止蒙面規例》合

"憲"，然而，這並不意味著《緊急條例》本身不存在問題。因為該條例是在一百年前制定的，自身存在明顯的缺陷，應及時加以完善。完善《緊急條例》的首要工作，是規制香港特區行政長官緊急立法權。鑒於英國的緊急立法比較先進，且香港特區與英國在法制方面存在密切的歷史淵源關係，香港特區《緊急條例》的完善，在具體內容上可以借鑒英國《國民緊急應變法（2004）》。當然，香港畢竟已經回歸中國，並成為中國管轄下的一個特別行政區，這決定了香港特區的緊急立法亦不能生搬硬套英國的模式，而必須充分考慮香港特別行政區自己的實際情況，並認清香港在國家體系中所處的地位和香港緊急情況的地方層級屬性。故此，香港特區《緊急條例》的修改和完善必須符合"一國兩制"和《香港基本法》等憲制文件的規定。借鑒英國《國民緊急應變法（2004）》，以完善香港特區《緊急條例》的具體內容應包括以下三個方面：列明緊急法對於相對人權利保障的具體可行措施，規範以行政長官為主導的緊急權模式，以及完善香港《緊急條例》的文本。

參考文獻

一、著作類

[1] （古希臘）亞里士多德：《政治學》，吳壽彭譯，北京：商
務印書館 2011 年版。

[2] （美）路易士·亨金：《權利的時代》，信春鷹等譯，北京：
知識出版社 1997 年版。

[3] （美）羅斯托：《憲法專政：現代民主國家中的危機政府》，
孟濤譯，北京：華夏出版社 2015 年版。

[4] （美）亞瑟·奧肯：《平等與效率》，王奔洲譯，北京：華
夏出版社 1987 年版。

[5] （英）洛克：《政府論：下冊》，葉啟芳、瞿菊農譯，北京：
商務印書館 2004 年版。

[6] 陳弘毅：《香港特別行政區的法治軌跡》，北京：中國民主
法制出版社 2010 年版。

[7] 陳璿：《緊急權體系建構與基本原理》，北京：北京大學出
版社 2021 年版。

[8]　郭春明：《緊急狀態法律制度研究》，北京：中國檢察出版社 2004 年版。

[9]　馬懷德：《應急反應的法學思考 ——"非典"法律問題研究》，北京：中國政法大學出版社 2004 年版。

[10]　孟濤：《中國非常法律研究》，北京：清華大學出版社 2012 年版。

[11]　戚建剛：《中國行政應急法律制度研究》，北京：北京大學出版社 2010 年版。

[12]　王旭坤：《緊急不避法治》，北京：法律出版社 2009 年版。

[13]　王禛軍：《國家緊急權的理論與實踐》，北京：法律出版社 2015 年版。

[14]　徐高、莫紀宏編著：《外國緊急狀態法律制度》，北京：法律出版社 1994 年版。

[15]　楊奇主編：《香港概論》（下），北京：中國社會科學出版社 1996 年版。

[16]　C. Rossiter, *Constitutional Dictatorship*, Princeton University Press, 1948.

[17]　Jack Simson Caird, Robert Hazell and Dawn Oliver, *The Constitutional Standards of the House of Lords Select Committee on the Constitution*, the Constitution Unit in School of Public Policy, University College London, 2015.

[18]　Mary Harris and David Wilson, *Parliamentary Practice in New Zealand*, Auckland: Oratia Media Ltd, 2017.

[19]　Yash Ghai, *Hong Kong's New Constitutional Order*, Hong

Kong University Press, 1999.

二、論文類

[1]　蔡定劍：《立法權與立法權限》，載《法學研究》1993 年第 5 期。

[2]　陳弘毅：《香港的憲政發展：從殖民地到特別行政區》，載《洪範評論》第 12 輯。

[3]　陳文敏：《香港人權法案生效首年的回顧》，載《法學評論》1992 年第 4 期。

[4]　陳祖為：《解釋〈基本法〉護法轉調 行政主導非〈基本法〉立法原意》，載《明報》2004 年 6 月 28 日。

[5]　陳佐洱：《設立香港特別行政區終審法院的中英談判》，載《縱橫》2012 年第 8 期。

[6]　程介南：《對基本法政治體制的探討》，載蕭蔚雲：《香港基本法的成功實踐》，北京：北京大學出版社 2000 年版。

[7]　底高揚：《論香港特別行政區行政長官的緊急立法權》，載《港澳研究》2021 年第 2 期。

[8]　郭道暉：《論國家立法權》，載《中外法學》1994 年第 4 期。

[9]　胡錦光：《論香港基本法審查權及其界限》，載《武漢大學學報》2017 年第 6 期。

[10]　姜明安：《突發事件下行政權力的規範》，載《法制日報》2003 年 5 月 15 日。

[11]　李樹忠、姚國建：《香港特區法院的違基審查權 —— 兼與董立坤、張淑鈿二位教授商榷》，載《法學研究》2012 年

第 2 期。

[12] 林鴻潮、周智博：《地方人大常委會緊急性授權的合憲性考察及其完善》，載《貴州社會科學》2020 年第 10 期。

[13] 劉恆：《論行政立法權》，載《法學評論》1995 年第 4 期。

[14] 劉兆佳：《行政主導的政治體制 —— 設想與現實》，載中央人民政府駐香港特別行政區聯絡辦公室：《關於 "一國兩制" 和香港問題的理論文集》。

[15] 羅昶、喬克裕、高其才：《論香港法的淵源》，載《法學評論》1997 年第 4 期。

[16] 呂景勝：《〈緊急狀態法〉立法研究》，載《中國人民大學學報》2003 年第 5 期。

[17] 莫紀宏：《緊急狀態入憲的意義》，載《法學家》2004 年第 4 期。

[18] 邵善波：《成文憲法對香港原有司法體制的影響》，載《港澳研究》2007 年冬季號。

[19] 汪超：《表達自由的邊界與基本法的解釋：從香港三級法院〈禁蒙面法〉相關判決看香港基本法的本地適用》，載《法律適用》2021 年第 4 期。

[20] 王磊：《香港政治體制應當表述為 "行政長官制"》，載《政治與法律》2016 年第 12 期。

[21] 王禎軍：《論行政緊急權的憲法規制》，載《河北法學》2017 年第 7 期。

[22] 蕭金明：《香港行政法制的啟示 —— 香港法治行政的觀察和聯想》，載《山東大學學報》2001 年第 1 期。

[23] 楊海坤：《對香港行政法的觀察與思考》，載《行政法學研究》1996 年第 1 期。

[24] 楊建平：《論香港實行行政主導的客觀必然性》，載《中國行政管理》2007 年第 10 期。

[25] 葉建民：《回顧歷史：這個錯誤真的有用嗎？》，載《明報》2019 年 10 月 11 日。

[26] Ann D. Jordan, "Lost in the Translation: Two Legal Cultures, the Common Law Judiciary and the Baic Law of the Hong Kong Special Administrative Region", *Cornell International Law Journal*, volume 30.

[27] Hualing Fu and Xiaobo Zhai, "Two Paradigms of Emergency Power: Hong Kong's Liberal Order Meeting the Authoritarian State", *Hong Kong Law Journal*, volume 50, part 2, 2020.

[28] James Chalmers and Fiona Leverick, "Criminal Law in the Shadows: Creating Offences in Delegated Legislation", *Legal Studies*, volume 38, 2018.

[29] Mirko Pečarič, "An Old Absolutist Amending Clause as the 'New' Instrument of Delegated Legislation", *The Theory and Practice of Legislation*, volume 4, 2016.

三、法律文件類

[1] 《關於訂定內部規範的法律制度》，澳門特別行政區立法會第 13/2009 號法律彙編。

[2] 《緊急情況規例條例》，由 1999 年第 71 號第 2 條修訂。

[3] 《經濟、社會與文化權利國際公約》（A 公約）、《公民權利和政治權利國際公約》（B 公約）和《公民權利和政治權利國際公約任擇議定書》（B 公約議定書），1966 年 12 月 16 日在第二十一屆聯合國大會上通過。

[4] 《釋義及通則條例》，由 2017 年第 1 號編輯修訂。

[5] *Civil Contingencies Act* 2004.

[6] Human Rights Committee, Comment No. 29: *States of Emergency* (Article 4), CCPR/C/21/Rev.1/Add.11.

四、網絡文章類

[1] 《〈禁止蒙面規例〉出臺後，誰慌了？》，http://www.bjd.com.cn/a/201910/14/WS5da3c5bee4b0ed1b67c5aba4.html（最後登錄日期：2020 年 4 月 23 日）。

[2] 《港府引用 "緊急法" 開先例，外界憂隨時 "加辣"》，https://www.rfa.org/cantonese/news/htm/hk-emergency-10042019094047.html（最後登錄日期：2019 年 12 月 10 日）。

[3] 《關於香港特別行政區實行 "三權分立" 的說法必須糾正》，https://baijiahao.baidu.com/s?id=167719174409749362 4&wfr=spider&for=pc（最後登錄日期：2022 年 10 月 3 日）。

[4] 《香港 "禁蒙面法" 無效？全國人大、國務院港澳辦表態！》，https://www.163.com/dy/article/EUCRL2QN055040N3.html（最後登錄日期：2022 年 10 月 12 日）。

[5] 《英國提出"緊急應變與復原準則"強化災難時之應變規定》，https://stli.iii.org.tw/article-detail.aspx?no=64&tp=1&d=6528（最後登錄日期：2022 年 12 月 1 日）。

[6] 李潤田：《各國如何應對緊急狀態》，http://www.people.com.cn/GB/junshi/1078/2948705.html?5ovxi（最後登錄日期：2020 年 12 月 2 日）。

[7] 張明楷：《法律不是被嘲笑的對象 —— 犯罪最大化的發展》，www.law-lib.com/flsz/sz_view.asp？no=2253（最後登錄日期：2020 年 3 月 18 日）。

[8] "Subordinate Legislation", https://www.parliament.scot/visitandlearn/100539.aspx (last accessed on 27 November 2019).

[9] "Understanding UK Legislation", https://www.soas.ac.uk/library/subjects/law/research/file70251.pdf (last accessed on 8 December 2019).

附錄一

香港特區 《緊急情況規例條例》

（本法例引自香港特區立法會網站，詳見：https://www. elegislation.gov.hk/hk/cap241；許可使用文件所在鏈接如下： https://www.elegislation.gov.hk/copyright。）

本條例旨在授予行政長官會同行政會議在緊急或危害公安的情況時訂立規例的權力。

（由 1999 年第 71 號第 3 條修訂）

[1922 年 2 月 28 日]

（格式變更——2018 年第 5 號編輯修訂紀錄）

1. 簡稱 本條例可引稱為《緊急情況規例條例》。

2. 訂立規例的權力

（1）在行政長官會同行政會議認為屬緊急情況或危害公安的情況時，行政長官會同行政會議可訂立任何他認為合乎公眾利益的規例。

（2）在不損害第（1）款條文的一般性的原則下，該等規例可就下列事項作出規定——（由 1924 年第 5 號第 9 條修訂；由 1949 年第 8 號第 2 條修訂）

（a）對刊物、文字、地圖、圖則、照片、通訊及通訊方法的檢查、管制及壓制；

（b）逮捕、羈留、驅逐及遞解離境；

（c）對香港的海港、港口及香港水域和對船隻移動的管制；

（d）陸路、航空或水上運輸，以及對運送人及東西的管制；

（e）貿易、出口、進口、生產及製造；

（f）對財產及其使用作出的撥配、管制、沒收及處置；

（g）修訂任何成文法則，暫停實施任何成文法則，以及應用任何不論是否經修改的成文法則；（由 1949 年第 8 號第 2 條代替）

（h）授權進入與搜查處所；（由 1949 年第 8 號第 2 條代替）

（i）賦權該等規例指明的主管當局或人士訂立命令及規則，並賦權他們為施行該等規例製備或發出通知書、牌照、許可證、證明書或其他文件；（由 1949 年第 8 號第 2 條代替）

（j）就為施行該等規例而批給或發出任何牌照、許可證、證明書或其他文件，收取該等規例訂明的費用；（由 1949 年第 8 號第 2 條增補）

（k）代表行政長官取得任何財產或業務的管有或控制；（由 1949 年第 8 號第 2 條增補）

（l）規定某些人進行工作或提供服務；（由 1949 年第 8 號第 2 條增補）

（m）向受該等規例影響的人支付補償及報酬，以及就上述補償作出決定；及（由 1949 年第 8 號第 2 條增補）

（n）對違反該等規例或任何在香港施行的法律的人的拘捕、審訊及懲罰，（由 1949 年第 8 號第 2 條增補。由 1949 年第 40 號第 2 條修訂）

並可載有行政長官覺得為施行該等規例而屬必需或合宜的附帶條文及補充條文。（由 1949 年第 8 號第 2 條增補）

（3）根據本條條文訂立的任何規例，須持續有效至行政長官會同行政會議藉命令廢除為止。

（4）任何規例或依據該規例訂立的命令或規則，即使與任何成文法則中所載者有抵觸，仍具效力；而任何成文法則中任何條文如與任何規例或任何上述命令或規則有抵觸，則不論該條文是否在其實施過程中已根據第（2）款予以修訂、暫停或修改，只要上述規例、命令或規則仍屬有效，上述有抵觸之處並無效力。（由 1949 年第 8 號第 2 條增補）

（5）每份看來是由行政長官或其他主管當局或人士依據本條例或依據任何根據本條例訂立的規例製備或發出的文書的文件，且該份文件看來是由行政長官或上述其他主管當局或人士或代表行政長官或上述其他主管當局或人士簽署，均須獲收取為證據，並在相反證明成立之前，須當作是由行政長官或該主管當局或人士製備或發出的文書。（由 1949 年第 8 號第 2 條增補）

（由 1999 年第 71 號第 3 條修訂）

3. 罰則

（1）在不損害第 2 條所授予的權力的原則下，根據本條例訂立的規例可就任何罪行（不論該罪行屬違反該等規例的罪行或屬任何適用於香港的法律所訂的罪行），規定以任何刑罰及制裁（包括強制性終身監禁的最高刑罰，但不包括死刑）作為該罪行的懲罰，並可載有關於沒收、處置與保留在任何方面與上述罪行有關的物品的條文，以及關於撤銷或取消根據該等規例或任何其他成文法則發出的牌照、許可證、通行證或許可權文件的條文，而該等刑罰、制裁及條文是行政長官會同行政會議覺得為確保任何規例或法律的強制執行而屬必需或合宜的，或在其他方面符合公眾利益的。（由 1993 年第 24 號第 24 條修訂；由 1999 年第 71 號第 3 條修訂）

（2）任何人如違反任何根據本條例訂立的規例，而該等規例並無規定其他刑罰或懲罰，則一經循簡易程序定罪，可處第 2 級罰款及監禁 2 年。（編輯修訂 —— 2021 年第 5 號編輯修訂紀錄）

（3）（由 1993 年第 24 號第 24 條廢除）

（由 1949 年第 40 號第 3 條代替）

4. 關於修訂條例效力的聲明條文

為免除疑問，特此聲明：第 2 條第（1）款中"行政長官會同行政會議可訂立任何他認為合乎公眾利益的規例"的字句，須當作一向包括訂立第 2 條第（2）款（g）段所述規例的權力，另又聲明：第 2 條第（4）款的條文，須當作一向已收納在本條例中。

（將 1949 年第 40 號第 4 條編入。

由 1999 年第 71 號第 3 條修訂）

附錄二

英國 《國民緊急應變法 (2004)》

（本法例引自英國立法機關網站，詳見：https://www.legislation.gov.uk/ukpga/2004/36/data.pdf；許可使用文件所在鏈接如下：https://www.nationalarchives.gov.uk/doc/open-government-licence/version/3/。）

附錄二　英國《國民緊急應變法（2004）》

Civil Contingencies Act 2004

2004 CHAPTER 36

An Act to make provision about civil contingencies.   [18th November 2004]

BE IT ENACTED by the Queen's most Excellent Majesty, by and with the advice and consent of the Lords Spiritual and Temporal, and Commons, in this present Parliament assembled, and by the authority of the same, as follows:—

PART 1

LOCAL ARRANGEMENTS FOR CIVIL PROTECTION

Introductory

1   **Meaning of "emergency"**

(1) In this Part "emergency" means—

    (a) an event or situation which threatens serious damage to human welfare in a place in the United Kingdom,

    (b) an event or situation which threatens serious damage to the environment of a place in the United Kingdom, or

    (c) war, or terrorism, which threatens serious damage to the security of the United Kingdom.

(2) For the purposes of subsection (1)(a) an event or situation threatens damage to human welfare only if it involves, causes or may cause—

    (a) loss of human life,

    (b) human illness or injury,

    (c) homelessness,

    (d) damage to property,

    (e) disruption of a supply of money, food, water, energy or fuel,

    (f) disruption of a system of communication,

2

Civil Contingencies Act 2004 (c. 36)
Part 1 – Local Arrangements for Civil Protection
Document Generated: 2022-08-21

*Changes to legislation: Civil Contingencies Act 2004 is up to date with all changes known to be in force on or before
21 August 2022. There are changes that may be brought into force at a future date. Changes that have been made
appear in the content and are referenced with annotations. (See end of Document for details) View outstanding changes*

    (g)   disruption of facilities for transport, or

    (h)   disruption of services relating to health.

(3) For the purposes of subsection (1)(b) an event or situation threatens damage to the environment only if it involves, causes or may cause—

    (a)   contamination of land, water or air with biological, chemical or radio-active matter, or

    (b)   disruption or destruction of plant life or animal life.

(4) A Minister of the Crown, or, in relation to Scotland, the Scottish Ministers, may by order—

    (a)   provide that a specified event or situation, or class of event or situation, is to be treated as falling, or as not falling, within any of paragraphs (a) to (c) of subsection (1);

    (b)   amend subsection (2) so as to provide that in so far as an event or situation involves or causes disruption of a specified supply, system, facility or service—

        (i) it is to be treated as threatening damage to human welfare, or

        (ii) it is no longer to be treated as threatening damage to human welfare.

[**F1**(4A) In relation to Northern Ireland, the power to make orders—

    (a)   under subsection (4)(a) in relation to subsection (1)(a) or (b), and

    (b)   under subsection (4)(b),

is exercisable by the Department of Justice in Northern Ireland (and not by a Minister of the Crown).]

(5) The event or situation mentioned in subsection (1) may occur or be inside or outside the United Kingdom.

Textual Amendments

F1   S. 1(4A) inserted (12.4.2010) by The Northern Ireland Act 1998 (Devolution of Policing and Justice Functions) Order 2010 (S.I. 2010/976), arts. 1(2), 5, **Sch. 3 para. 95(2)** (with arts. 28-31, Sch. 3 para. 110)

Commencement Information

I1   S. 1 wholly in force at 14.11.2005; s. 1 not in force at Royal Assent, see s. 34; s. 1(1)-(3)(5) in force at 14.11.2005 by S.I. 2005/2040, **art. 3(a)**; s. 1(4) in force at 14.11.2005 by S.I. 2005/2040, **art. 3(a)** and S.S.I. 2005/493, **art. 4(a)**

Contingency planning

2   **Duty to assess, plan and advise**

(1) A person or body listed in [**F2**Part 1, 2 or 2A of Schedule 1] shall—

    (a)   from time to time assess the risk of an emergency occurring,

    (b)   from time to time assess the risk of an emergency making it necessary or expedient for the person or body to perform any of his or its functions,

Civil Contingencies Act 2004 (c. 36)
Part 1 – Local Arrangements for Civil Protection
Document Generated: 2022-08-21

3

(c) maintain plans for the purpose of ensuring, so far as is reasonably practicable, that if an emergency occurs the person or body is able to continue to perform his or its functions,

(d) maintain plans for the purpose of ensuring that if an emergency occurs or is likely to occur the person or body is able to perform his or its functions so far as necessary or desirable for the purpose of—

    (i) preventing the emergency,

    (ii) reducing, controlling or mitigating its effects, or

    (iii) taking other action in connection with it,

(e) consider whether an assessment carried out under paragraph (a) or (b) makes it necessary or expedient for the person or body to add to or modify plans maintained under paragraph (c) or (d),

(f) arrange for the publication of all or part of assessments made and plans maintained under paragraphs (a) to (d) in so far as publication is necessary or desirable for the purpose of—

    (i) preventing an emergency,

    (ii) reducing, controlling or mitigating the effects of an emergency, or

    (iii) enabling other action to be taken in connection with an emergency, and

(g) maintain arrangements to warn the public, and to provide information and advice to the public, if an emergency is likely to occur or has occurred.

(2) In relation to a person or body listed in [F3Part 1, 2 or 2A of Schedule 1] a duty in subsection (1) applies in relation to an emergency only if—

(a) the emergency would be likely seriously to obstruct the person or body in the performance of his or its functions, or

(b) it is likely that the person or body—

    (i) would consider it necessary or desirable to take action to prevent the emergency, to reduce, control or mitigate its effects or otherwise in connection with it, and

    (ii) would be unable to take that action without changing the deployment of resources or acquiring additional resources.

(3) A Minister of the Crown may, in relation to a person or body listed in Part 1 of Schedule 1, make regulations about—

(a) the extent of a duty under subsection (1) (subject to subsection (2));

(b) the manner in which a duty under subsection (1) is to be performed.

(4) The Scottish Ministers may, in relation to a person or body listed in Part 2 of Schedule 1, make regulations about—

(a) the extent of a duty under subsection (1) (subject to subsection (2));

(b) the manner in which a duty under subsection (1) is to be performed.

[F4(4A) The Welsh Ministers may, in relation to a person or body listed in Part 2A of Schedule 1, make regulations about—

(a) the extent of a duty under subsection (1) (subject to subsection (2));

(b) the manner in which a duty under subsection (1) is to be performed.]

(5) Regulations under subsection (3) may, in particular—

(a) make provision about the kind of emergency in relation to which a specified person or body is or is not to perform a duty under subsection (1);

Changes to legislation: Civil Contingencies Act 2004 is up to date with all changes known to be in force on or before 21 August 2022. There are changes that may be brought into force at a future date. Changes that have been made appear in the content and are referenced with annotations. (See end of Document for details) View outstanding changes

(b) permit or require a person or body not to perform a duty under subsection (1) in specified circumstances or in relation to specified matters;

(c) make provision as to the timing of performance of a duty under subsection (1);

(d) require a person or body to consult a specified person or body or class of person or body before or in the course of performing a duty under subsection (1);

(e) permit or require a county council to perform a duty under subsection (1) on behalf of a district council within the area of the county council;

(f) permit, require or prohibit collaboration, to such extent and in such manner as may be specified, by persons or bodies in the performance of a duty under subsection (1);

(g) permit, require or prohibit delegation, to such extent and in such manner as may be specified, of the performance of a duty under subsection (1);

(h) permit or require a person or body listed in Part 1 or 3 of Schedule 1 to co-operate, to such extent and in such manner as may be specified, with a person or body listed in Part 1 of the Schedule in connection with the performance of a duty under subsection (1);

(i) permit or require a person or body listed in Part 1 or 3 of Schedule 1 to provide information, either on request or in other specified circumstances, to a person or body listed in Part 1 of the Schedule in connection with the performance of a duty under subsection (1);

(j) permit or require a person or body to perform (wholly or partly) a duty under subsection (1)(a) or (b) having regard to, or by adopting or relying on, work undertaken by another specified person or body;

(k) permit or require a person or body, in maintaining a plan under subsection (1) (c) or (d), to have regard to the activities of bodies (other than public or local authorities) whose activities are not carried on for profit;

(l) make provision about the extent of, and the degree of detail to be contained in, a plan maintained under subsection (1)(c) or (d);

(m) require a plan to include provision for the carrying out of exercises;

(n) require a plan to include provision for the training of staff or other persons;

(o) permit a person or body to make arrangements with another person or body, as part of planning undertaken under subsection (1)(c) or (d), for the performance of a function on behalf of the first person or body;

(p) confer a function on a Minister of the Crown, on the Scottish Ministers, on the National Assembly for Wales, on a Northern Ireland department or on any other specified person or body (and a function conferred may, in particular, be a power or duty to exercise a discretion);

(q) make provision which has effect despite other provision made by or by virtue of an enactment;

(r) make provision which applies generally or only to a specified person or body or only in specified circumstances;

(s) make different provision for different persons or bodies or for different circumstances.

(6) Subsection (5) shall have effect in relation to subsection (4) as it has effect in relation to subsection (3), but as if—

(a) paragraph (e) were omitted,

(b) in paragraphs (h) and (i)—

Changes to legislation: Civil Contingencies Act 2004 is up to date with all changes known to be in force on or before
21 August 2022. There are changes that may be brought into force at a future date. Changes that have been made
appear in the content and are referenced with annotations. (See end of Document for details) View outstanding changes

(i) a reference to Part 1 or 3 of Schedule 1 were a reference to Part 2 or 4 of that Schedule, and

(ii) a reference to Part 1 of that Schedule were a reference to Part 2 of that Schedule, and

(c) in paragraph (p) the references to a Minister of the Crown, to the National Assembly for Wales and to a Northern Ireland department were omitted.

[**F5**(6A) Subsection (5) has effect in relation to subsection (4A) as it has effect in relation to subsection (3), but as if—

(a) paragraph (e) were omitted,

(b) in paragraphs (h) and (i)—

(i) a reference to Part 1 or 3 of Schedule 1 were a reference to Part 2A or 5 of that Schedule, and

(ii) a reference to Part 1 of that Schedule were a reference to Part 2A of that Schedule, and

(c) in paragraph (p) the references to a Minister of the Crown, the Scottish Ministers and a Northern Ireland department were omitted.]

[**F6**(7) In relation to emergencies that do not fall within section 1(1)(c), the power under subsection (3) to make regulations in relation to the Chief Constable (PSNI) is exercisable by the Department of Justice in Northern Ireland (and not by a Minister of the Crown).

(8) Subsection (5) has effect in relation to the power of the Department of Justice under subsection (3) as if—

(a) paragraphs (e), (h) and (i) were omitted;

(b) in paragraph (p) for the words from "a Minister of the Crown" to "department" there were substituted a Northern Ireland department.

(9) In relation to emergencies that do not fall within section 1(1)(c), a Minister of the Crown has no power by virtue of subsection (5)(h) or (i) to make provision permitting or requiring the Chief Constable (PSNI) to co-operate with, or provide information to, a person or body listed in Part 1 of Schedule 1.]

Textual Amendments

F2 Words in s. 2(1) substituted (24.5.2018) by The Welsh Ministers (Transfer of Functions) Order 2018 (S.I. 2018/644), arts. 1(1), **41(2)(a)**

F3 Words in s. 2(2) substituted (24.5.2018) by The Welsh Ministers (Transfer of Functions) Order 2018 (S.I. 2018/644), arts. 1(1), **41(2)(a)**

F4 S. 2(4A) inserted (24.5.2018) by The Welsh Ministers (Transfer of Functions) Order 2018 (S.I. 2018/644), arts. 1(1), **41(2)(b)**

F5 S. 2(6A) inserted (24.5.2018) by The Welsh Ministers (Transfer of Functions) Order 2018 (S.I. 2018/644), arts. 1(1), **41(2)(c)**

F6 S. 2(7)-(9) inserted (12.4.2010) by The Northern Ireland Act 1998 (Devolution of Policing and Justice Functions) Order 2010 (S.I. 2010/976), arts. 1(2), 5, **Sch. 3 para. 96(2)** (with arts. 28-31, Sch. 3 para. 110)

Commencement Information

I2 S. 2 partly in force; s. 2 not in force at Royal Assent see s. 34; s. 2(3)(5) in force for specified purposes at 22.7.2005 and s. 2(1)(2) in force for specified purposes at 14.11.2005 by S.I. 2005/2040, **arts. 2(a)**,

6

Civil Contingencies Act 2004 (c. 36)
Part 1 – Local Arrangements for Civil Protection
Document Generated: 2022-08-21

Changes to legislation: Civil Contingencies Act 2004 is up to date with all changes known to be in force on or before
21 August 2022. There are changes that may be brought into force at a future date. Changes that have been made
appear in the content and are referenced with annotations. (See end of Document for details) View outstanding changes

3(b); s. 2(4)(6) in force and s. 2(5) in force for specified purposes (S.) at 6.10.2005 and s. 2(1)(2) in force for further specified purposes (S.) at 14.11.2005 by S.S.I. 2005/493, **arts. 3(a)(b), 4(a)(b)**

3 Section 2: supplemental

(1) A Minister of the Crown may issue guidance to a person or body listed in Part 1 or 3 of Schedule 1 about the matters specified in section 2(3) and (5).

(2) The Scottish Ministers may issue guidance to a person or body listed in Part 2 or 4 of Schedule 1 about the matters specified in section 2(4) and (5) (as applied by section 2(6)).

[F7(2A) The Welsh Ministers may issue guidance to a person or body listed in Part 2A or 5 of Schedule 1 about the matters specified in section 2(4A) and (5) (as applied by section 2(6A)).]

(3) A person or body listed in any Part of Schedule 1 shall—

    (a)   comply with regulations under [F8section 2(3), (4) or (4A)] , and
    (b)   have regard to guidance under [F9subsection (1), (2) or (2A)] above.

(4) A person or body listed in [F10Part 1, 2 or 2A of] Schedule 1 may be referred to as a "Category 1 responder".

(5) A person or body listed in [F11Part 3, 4 or 5 of] Schedule 1 may be referred to as a "Category 2 responder".

[F12(6) In relation to emergencies that do not fall within section 1(1)(c), the power under subsection (1) to issue guidance to the Chief Constable (PSNI) is exercisable by the Department of Justice in Northern Ireland (and not by a Minister of the Crown).]

Textual Amendments

F7   S. 3(2A) inserted (24.5.2018) by The Welsh Ministers (Transfer of Functions) Order 2018 (S.I. 2018/644), arts. 1(1), **41(3)(a)**

F8   Words in s. 3(3)(a) substituted (24.5.2018) by The Welsh Ministers (Transfer of Functions) Order 2018 (S.I. 2018/644), arts. 1(1), **41(3)(b)**

F9   Words in s. 3(3)(b) substituted (24.5.2018) by The Welsh Ministers (Transfer of Functions) Order 2018 (S.I. 2018/644), arts. 1(1), **41(3)(c)**

F10 Words in s. 3(4) substituted (24.5.2018) by The Welsh Ministers (Transfer of Functions) Order 2018 (S.I. 2018/644), arts. 1(1), **41(3)(d)**

F11 Words in s. 3(5) substituted (24.5.2018) by The Welsh Ministers (Transfer of Functions) Order 2018 (S.I. 2018/644), arts. 1(1), **41(3)(e)**

F12 S. 3(6) inserted (12.4.2010) by The Northern Ireland Act 1998 (Devolution of Policing and Justice Functions) Order 2010 (S.I. 2010/976), arts. 1(2), 5, **Sch. 3 para. 97(2)** (with arts. 28-31, Sch. 3 para. 110)

Commencement Information

I3   S. 3 partly in force; s. 3 not in force at Royal Assent see s. 34; s. 3(1)(3)(4)(5) in force for specified purposes at 14.11.2005 by S.I. 2005/2040, **art. 3(c)**; s. 3(2) in force and s. 3(4)(5) in force for specified purposes (S.) at 6.10.2005 and s. 3(3) in force for specified purposes (S.) at 14.11.2005 by S.S.I. 2005/493, **arts. 3(c)(d), 4(c)**

Changes to legislation: Civil Contingencies Act 2004 is up to date with all changes known to be in force on or before
21 August 2022. There are changes that may be brought into force at a future date. Changes that have been made
appear in the content and are referenced with annotations. (See end of Document for details) View outstanding changes

4   Advice and assistance to the public

(1) A body specified in [F13paragraph 1, 13 or 18A] of Schedule 1 shall provide advice and assistance to the public in connection with the making of arrangements for the continuance of commercial activities by the public, or the continuance of the activities of bodies other than public or local authorities whose activities are not carried on for profit, in the event of an emergency.

(2) A Minister of the Crown may, in relation to a body specified in [F14paragraph 1] of that Schedule, make regulations about—

    (a)   the extent of the duty under subsection (1);

    (b)   the manner in which the duty under subsection (1) is to be performed.

(3) The Scottish Ministers may, in relation to a body specified in paragraph 13 of that Schedule, make regulations about—

    (a)   the extent of the duty under subsection (1);

    (b)   the manner in which the duty under subsection (1) is to be performed.

[F15(3A) The Welsh Ministers may, in relation to a body specified in paragraph 18A of that Schedule, make regulations about—

    (a)   the extent of the duty under subsection (1);

    (b)   the manner in which the duty under subsection (1) is to be performed.]

(4) Regulations under [F16subsection (2), (3) or (3A)] may, in particular—

    (a)   permit a body to make a charge for advice or assistance provided on request under subsection (1);

    (b)   make provision of a kind permitted to be made by regulations under section 2(5)(a) to (i) and (o) to (s).

(5) Regulations by virtue of subsection (4)(a) must provide that a charge for advice or assistance may not exceed the aggregate of—

    (a)   the direct costs of providing the advice or assistance, and

    (b)   a reasonable share of any costs indirectly related to the provision of the advice or assistance.

(6) A Minister of the Crown may issue guidance to a body specified in [F17paragraph 1] of that Schedule about the matters specified in subsections (2) and (4).

(7) The Scottish Ministers may issue guidance to a body specified in paragraph 13 of that Schedule about the matters specified in subsections (3) and (4).

[F18(7A) The Welsh Ministers may issue guidance to a body specified in paragraph 18A of that Schedule about the matters specified in subsections (3A) and (4).]

(8) A body shall—

    (a)   comply with regulations under [F19subsection (2), (3) or (3A)] , and

    (b)   have regard to guidance under [F20subsection (6), (7) or (7A)] .

Textual Amendments

F13 Words in s. 4(1) substituted (24.5.2018) by The Welsh Ministers (Transfer of Functions) Order 2018 (S.I. 2018/644), arts. 1(1), **41(4)(a)**

F14 Words in s. 4(2) substituted (24.5.2018) by The Welsh Ministers (Transfer of Functions) Order 2018 (S.I. 2018/644), arts. 1(1), **41(4)(b)**

8

Civil Contingencies Act 2004 (c. 36)
Part 1 – Local Arrangements for Civil Protection
Document Generated: 2022-08-21

Changes to legislation: Civil Contingencies Act 2004 is up to date with all changes known to be in force on or before 21 August 2022. There are changes that may be brought into force at a future date. Changes that have been made appear in the content and are referenced with annotations. (See end of Document for details) View outstanding changes

F15   S. 4(3A) inserted (24.5.2018) by The Welsh Ministers (Transfer of Functions) Order 2018 (S.I. 2018/644), arts. 1(1), **41(4)(c)**

F16   Words in s. 4(4) substituted (24.5.2018) by The Welsh Ministers (Transfer of Functions) Order 2018 (S.I. 2018/644), arts. 1(1), **41(4)(d)**

F17   Words in s. 4(6) substituted (24.5.2018) by The Welsh Ministers (Transfer of Functions) Order 2018 (S.I. 2018/644), arts. 1(1), **41(4)(e)**

F18   S. 4(7A) inserted (24.5.2018) by The Welsh Ministers (Transfer of Functions) Order 2018 (S.I. 2018/644), arts. 1(1), **41(4)(f)**

F19   Words in s. 4(8)(a) substituted (24.5.2018) by The Welsh Ministers (Transfer of Functions) Order 2018 (S.I. 2018/644), arts. 1(1), **41(4)(g)**

F20   Words in s. 4(8)(b) substituted (24.5.2018) by The Welsh Ministers (Transfer of Functions) Order 2018 (S.I. 2018/644), arts. 1(1), **41(4)(h)**

Commencement Information

I4   S. 4 partly in force; s. 4 not in force at Royal Assent see s. 34; s. 4(2)(4)(5) in force for specified purposes at 22.7.2005 and s. 4(1)(6)(8) in force for specified purposes at 14.11.2005 and s. 4(1)(2)(4)(5)(6)(8) in force for further specified purposes at 15.5.2006 by S.I. 2005/2040, **arts. 2(b), 3(d), 4**; s. 4(3)(7) in force and s. 4(4)(5) in force for specified purposes (S.) at 6.10.2005 and s. 4(1)(8) in force for further specified purposes (S.) at 14.11.2005 and s. 4(1) in force for further specified purposes (S.) at 15.5.2006 by S.S.I. 2005/493, **arts. 3(e)(f), 4(d)(e), 5**

Civil protection

5   **General measures**

(1) A Minister of the Crown may by order require a person or body listed in Part 1 of Schedule 1 to perform a function of that person or body for the purpose of—

    (a)   preventing the occurrence of an emergency,

    (b)   reducing, controlling or mitigating the effects of an emergency, or

    (c)   taking other action in connection with an emergency.

(2) The Scottish Ministers may by order require a person or body listed in Part 2 of Schedule 1 to perform a function of that person or body for the purpose of—

    (a)   preventing the occurrence of an emergency,

    (b)   reducing, controlling or mitigating the effects of an emergency, or

    (c)   taking other action in connection with an emergency.

[F21(2A) The Welsh Ministers may by order require a person or body listed in Part 2A of Schedule 1 to perform a function of that person or body for the purpose of—

    (a)   preventing the occurrence of an emergency,

    (b)   reducing, controlling or mitigating the effects of an emergency, or

    (c)   taking other action in connection with an emergency.]

(3) A person or body shall comply with an order under this section.

(4) An order under subsection (1) may—

    (a)   require a person or body to consult a specified person or body or class of person or body;

    (b)   permit, require or prohibit collaboration, to such extent and in such manner as may be specified;

Changes to legislation: Civil Contingencies Act 2004 is up to date with all changes known to be in force on or before
21 August 2022. There are changes that may be brought into force at a future date. Changes that have been made
appear in the content and are referenced with annotations. (See end of Document for details) View outstanding changes

(c)   permit, require or prohibit delegation, to such extent and in such manner as may be specified;

(d)   permit or require a person or body listed in Part 1 or 3 of Schedule 1 to co-operate, to such extent and in such manner as may be specified, with a person or body listed in Part 1 of the Schedule in connection with a duty under the order;

(e)   permit or require a person or body listed in Part 1 or 3 of Schedule 1 to provide information in connection with a duty under the order, whether on request or in other specific circumstances to a person or body listed in Part 1 of the Schedule;

(f)   confer a function on a Minister of the Crown, on the Scottish Ministers, on the National Assembly for Wales, on a Northern Ireland department or on any other specified person or body (and a function conferred may, in particular, be a power or duty to exercise a discretion);

(g)   make provision which applies generally or only to a specified person or body or only in specified circumstances;

(h)   make different provision for different persons or bodies or for different circumstances.

(5) Subsection (4) shall have effect in relation to subsection (2) as it has effect in relation to subsection (1), but as if—

(a)   in paragraphs (d) and (e)—

(i) a reference to Part 1 or 3 of Schedule 1 were a reference to Part 2 or 4 of that Schedule, and

(ii) a reference to Part 1 of that Schedule were a reference to Part 2 of that Schedule, and

(b)   in paragraph (f) the references to a Minister of the Crown, to the National Assembly for Wales and to a Northern Ireland department were omitted.

[F22(5A) Subsection (4) has effect in relation to subsection (2A) as it has effect in relation to subsection (1), but as if—

(a)   in paragraphs (d) and (e)—

(i) a reference to Part 1 or 3 of Schedule 1 were a reference to Part 2A or 5 of that Schedule, and

(ii) a reference to Part 1 of that Schedule were a reference to Part 2A of that Schedule, and

(b)   in paragraph (f) the references to a Minister of the Crown, to the Scottish Ministers and to a Northern Ireland department were omitted.]

[F23(6) In relation to emergencies that do not fall within section 1(1)(c), the power under subsection (1) to require the Chief Constable (PSNI) to perform a function is exercisable by the Department of Justice in Northern Ireland (and not by a Minister of the Crown).

(7) Subsection (4) has effect in relation to the power of the Department of Justice under subsection (1) as if—

(a)   paragraphs (d) and (e) were omitted;

(b)   in paragraph (f) for the words from "a Minister of the Crown" to "department" there were substituted a Northern Ireland department.

(8) In relation to emergencies that do not fall within section 1(1)(c), a Minister of the Crown has no power by virtue of subsection (4)(d) or (e) to make provision permitting

10

Civil Contingencies Act 2004 (c. 36)
Part 1 – Local Arrangements for Civil Protection
Document Generated: 2022-08-21

*Changes to legislation: Civil Contingencies Act 2004 is up to date with all changes known to be in force on or before
21 August 2022. There are changes that may be brought into force at a future date. Changes that have been made
appear in the content and are referenced with annotations. (See end of Document for details) View outstanding changes*

or requiring the Chief Constable (PSNI) to co-operate with, or provide information to, a person or body listed in Part 1 of Schedule 1.]

Textual Amendments

F21 S. 5(2A) inserted (24.5.2018) by The Welsh Ministers (Transfer of Functions) Order 2018 (S.I. 2018/644), arts. 1(1), **41(5)(a)**

F22 S. 5(5A) inserted (24.5.2018) by The Welsh Ministers (Transfer of Functions) Order 2018 (S.I. 2018/644), arts. 1(1), **41(5)(b)**

F23 S. 5(6)-(8) inserted (12.4.2010) by The Northern Ireland Act 1998 (Devolution of Policing and Justice Functions) Order 2010 (S.I. 2010/976), arts. 1(2), 5, **Sch. 3 para. 98(2)** (with arts. 28-31, Sch. 3 para. 110)

Commencement Information

I5 S. 5 partly in force; s. 5 not in force at Royal Assent see s. 34; s. 5(1)(3)(4) in force for specified purposes at 14.11.2005 by S.I. 2005/2040, **art. 3(e)**; s. 5(2)(5) in force and s. 5(3)(4) in force for further specified purposes (S.) at 14.11.2005 by S.S.I. 2005/493, **art. 4**

6   Disclosure of information

(1) A Minister of the Crown may make regulations requiring or permitting one person or body listed in Part 1 or 3 of Schedule 1 ("the provider") to disclose information on request to another person or body listed in any Part of that Schedule ("the recipient").

(2) The Scottish Ministers may make regulations requiring or permitting one person or body listed in Part 2 or 4 of Schedule 1 ("the provider") to disclose information on request to another person or body listed in any Part of that Schedule ("the recipient").

[F24(2A) The Welsh Ministers may make regulations requiring or permitting one person or body listed in Part 2A or 5 of Schedule 1 ("the provider") to disclose information on request to another person or body listed in any Part of that Schedule ("the recipient").]

(3) Regulations under [F25subsection (1), (2) or (2A)] may be made only in connection with a function of the provider or of the recipient which relates to emergencies.

(4) A Minister of the Crown may issue guidance to a person or body about the performance of functions under regulations made under subsection (1).

(5) The Scottish Ministers may issue guidance to a person or body about the performance of functions under regulations made under subsection (2).

[F26(5A) The Welsh Ministers may issue guidance to a person or body about the performance of functions under regulations made under subsection (2A).]

(6) A person or body shall—
    (a)   comply with regulations under [F27subsection (1), (2) or (2A)] , and
    (b)   have regard to guidance under [F28subsection (4), (5) or (5A)] .

[F29(7) In relation to emergencies that do not fall within section 1(1)(c), the following powers are exercisable by the Department of Justice in Northern Ireland (and not by a Minister of the Crown)—
    (a)   the power under subsection (1) to make regulations requiring or permitting the Chief Constable (PSNI) to disclose information to another person or body listed in any Part of Schedule 1;

Changes to legislation: Civil Contingencies Act 2004 is up to date with all changes known to be in force on or before
21 August 2022. There are changes that may be brought into force at a future date. Changes that have been made
appear in the content and are referenced with annotations. (See end of Document for details) View outstanding changes

(b) the power under subsection (4) to issue guidance to the Chief Constable (PSNI).]

Textual Amendments

F24 S. 6(2A) inserted (24.5.2018) by The Welsh Ministers (Transfer of Functions) Order 2018 (S.I. 2018/644), arts. 1(1), **41(6)(a)**

F25 Words in s. 6(3) substituted (24.5.2018) by The Welsh Ministers (Transfer of Functions) Order 2018 (S.I. 2018/644), arts. 1(1), **41(6)(b)**

F26 S. 6(5A) inserted (24.5.2018) by The Welsh Ministers (Transfer of Functions) Order 2018 (S.I. 2018/644), arts. 1(1), **41(6)(c)**

F27 Words in s. 6(6)(a) substituted (24.5.2018) by The Welsh Ministers (Transfer of Functions) Order 2018 (S.I. 2018/644), arts. 1(1), **41(6)(d)**

F28 Words in s. 6(6)(b) substituted (24.5.2018) by The Welsh Ministers (Transfer of Functions) Order 2018 (S.I. 2018/644), arts. 1(1), **41(6)(e)**

F29 S. 6(7) inserted (12.4.2010) by The Northern Ireland Act 1998 (Devolution of Policing and Justice Functions) Order 2010 (S.I. 2010/976), arts. 1(2), 5, **Sch. 3 para. 99(2)** (with arts. 28-31, Sch. 3 para. 110)

Commencement Information

I6 S. 6 partly in force; s. 6 not in force at Royal Assent see s. 34; s. 6(1) in force for specified purposes at 22.7.2005 and s. 6(3)(4)(6) in force for specified purposes at 14.11.2005 by S.I. 2005/2040, **arts. 2(c)**, 3(f); s. 6(2)(5) in force and s. 6(3) in force for specified purposes (S.) at 6.10.2005 and s. 6(6) in force for specified purposes (S.) at 14.11.2005 by S.S.I. 2005/493, **arts. 3(g)(h), 4(h)**

General

7 Urgency

(1) This section applies where—

    (a) there is an urgent need to make provision of a kind that could be made by an order under section 5(1) or by regulations under section 6(1), but

    (b) there is insufficient time for the order or regulations to be made.

(2) The Minister may by direction make provision of a kind that could be made by an order under section 5(1) or by regulations under section 6(1).

(3) A direction under subsection (2) shall be in writing.

(4) Where a Minister gives a direction under subsection (2)—

    (a) he may revoke or vary the direction by further direction,

    (b) he shall revoke the direction as soon as is reasonably practicable (and he may, if or in so far as he thinks it desirable, re-enact the substance of the direction by way of an order under section 5(1) or by way of regulations under section 6(1)), and

    (c) the direction shall cease to have effect at the end of the period of 21 days beginning with the day on which it is given (but without prejudice to the power to give a new direction).

[F30(4A) In relation to provision of a kind that could be made by the Department of Justice in Northern Ireland by an order under section 5(1) or by regulations under section 6(1),

12

Civil Contingencies Act 2004 (c. 36)
Part 1 – Local Arrangements for Civil Protection
Document Generated: 2022-08-21

in subsection (2) the reference to the Minister is to be read as a reference to the Department of Justice and subsection (4) is to be read accordingly.]

(5) A provision of a direction under subsection (2) shall be treated for all purposes as if it were a provision of an order under section 5(1) or of regulations under section 6(1) [F31made by the Minister or the Department of Justice (as the case may be)].

Textual Amendments

F30 S. 7(4A) inserted (12.4.2010) by The Northern Ireland Act 1998 (Devolution of Policing and Justice Functions) Order 2010 (S.I. 2010/976), arts. 1(2), 5, **Sch. 3 para. 100(2)** (with arts. 28-31, Sch. 3 para. 110)

F31 Words in s. 7(5) inserted (12.4.2010) by The Northern Ireland Act 1998 (Devolution of Policing and Justice Functions) Order 2010 (S.I. 2010/976), arts. 1(2), 5, **Sch. 3 para. 100(3)** (with arts. 28-31, Sch. 3 para. 110)

8   Urgency: Scotland

(1) This section applies where—

    (a)   there is an urgent need to make provision of a kind that could be made by an order under section 5(2) or by regulations under section 6(2), but

    (b)   there is insufficient time for the order or regulations to be made.

(2) The Scottish Ministers may by direction make provision of a kind that could be made by an order under section 5(2) or by regulations under section 6(2).

(3) A direction under subsection (2) shall be in writing.

(4) Where the Scottish Ministers give a direction under subsection (2)—

    (a)   they may revoke or vary the direction by further direction,

    (b)   they shall revoke the direction as soon as is reasonably practicable (and they may, if or in so far as they think it desirable, re-enact the substance of the direction by way of an order under section 5(2) or by way of regulations under section 6(2)), and

    (c)   the direction shall cease to have effect at the end of the period of 21 days beginning with the day on which it is given (but without prejudice to the power to give a new direction).

(5) A provision of a direction under subsection (2) shall be treated for all purposes as if it were a provision of an order under section 5(2) or of regulations under section 6(2).

Modifications etc. (not altering text)

C1 S. 8 partly in force; s. 8 not in force at Royal Assent see s. 34; s. 8 in force (S.) at 14.11.2005 by S.S.I. 2005/493, **art. 4**

[F32**8A. Urgency: Wales**

(1) This section applies where—

    (a)   there is an urgent need to make provision of the kind that could be made by an order under section 5(2A) or by regulations under section 6(2A), but

---

    (b)   there is insufficient time for the order or regulations to be made.

(2) The Welsh Ministers may by direction make provision of the kind that could be made by an order under section 5(2A) or by regulations under section 6(2A).

(3) A direction under subsection (2) must be in writing.

(4) Where the Welsh Ministers give a direction under subsection (2)—

    (a)   they may revoke or vary the direction by further direction,

    (b)   they must revoke the direction as soon as is reasonably practicable (and they may, if or in so far as they think it desirable, re-enact the substance of the direction by way of an order under section 5(2A) or by way of regulations under section 6(2A)), and

    (c)   the direction ceases to have effect at the end of the period of 21 days beginning with the day on which it is given (but without prejudice to the power to give a new direction).

(5) A provision of a direction under subsection (2) is to be treated for all purposes as if it were a provision of an order under section 5(2A) or of regulations under section 6(2A).]

Textual Amendments

F32 S. 8A inserted (24.5.2018) by The Welsh Ministers (Transfer of Functions) Order 2018 (S.I. 2018/644), arts. 1(1), 41(7)

9   **Monitoring by Government**

(1) A Minister of the Crown may require a person or body listed in Part 1 or 3 of Schedule 1—

    (a)   to provide information about action taken by the person or body for the purpose of complying with a duty under this Part, or

    (b)   to explain why the person or body has not taken action for the purpose of complying with a duty under this Part.

(2) The Scottish Ministers may require a person or body listed in Part 2 or 4 of Schedule 1—

    (a)   to provide information about action taken by the person or body for the purpose of complying with a duty under this Part, or

    (b)   to explain why the person or body has not taken action for the purpose of complying with a duty under this Part.

[F33(2A) The Welsh Ministers may require a person or body listed in Part 2A or 5 of Schedule 1—

    (a)   to provide information about action taken by the person or body for the purpose of complying with a duty under this Part, or

    (b)   to explain why the person or body has not taken action for the purpose of complying with a duty under this Part.]

(3) A requirement under [F34subsection (1), (2) or (2A)] may specify—

    (a)   a period within which the information or explanation is to be provided;

    (b)   the form in which the information or explanation is to be provided.

14

Civil Contingencies Act 2004 (c. 36)
Part 1 – Local Arrangements for Civil Protection
Document Generated: 2022-08-21

(4) A person or body shall comply with a requirement under [^{F35}subsection (1), (2) or (2A)] .

[^{F36}(5) In relation to emergencies that do not fall within section 1(1)(c), the power under subsection (1) to require the Chief Constable (PSNI) to provide information or an explanation is exercisable by the Department of Justice in Northern Ireland (and not by a Minister of the Crown).

(6) If it appears to the Chief Constable (PSNI) that a requirement imposed by virtue of subsection (5) may require the Chief Constable (PSNI) to provide national security information, the Chief Constable (PSNI) may refer the requirement to a Minister of the Crown.

(7) The Minister may set aside or otherwise modify the requirement as the Minister considers appropriate so that the Chief Constable (PSNI) is not required to provide any information which appears to the Minister to be national security information.

(8) "National security information" means information the disclosure of which to the public would, or would be likely to, adversely affect national security.]

Textual Amendments

F33 S. 9(2A) inserted (24.5.2018) by The Welsh Ministers (Transfer of Functions) Order 2018 (S.I. 2018/644), arts. 1(1), **41(8)(a)**

F34 Words in s. 9(3) substituted (24.5.2018) by The Welsh Ministers (Transfer of Functions) Order 2018 (S.I. 2018/644), arts. 1(1), **41(8)(b)**

F35 Words in s. 9(4) substituted (24.5.2018) by The Welsh Ministers (Transfer of Functions) Order 2018 (S.I. 2018/644), arts. 1(1), **41(8)(c)**

F36 S. 9(5)-(8) inserted (12.4.2010) by The Northern Ireland Act 1998 (Devolution of Policing and Justice Functions) Order 2010 (S.I. 2010/976), arts. 1(2), 5, **Sch. 3 para. 101(2)** (with arts. 28-31, Sch. 3 para. 110)

Commencement Information

I7 S. 9 partly in force; s. 9 not in force at Royal Assent see s. 34; s. 9(1)(3)(4) in force for specified purposes at 14.11.2005 by S.I. 2005/2040, **art. 3(h)**; s. 9(2) in force and s. 9(3)(4) in force for further specified purposes (S.) at 14.11.2005 by S.S.I. 2005/493, **art. 4**

10   Enforcement

(1) Any of the following may bring proceedings in the High Court or the Court of Session in respect of a failure by a person or body listed in Part 1 or 3 of Schedule 1 to comply with section 2(1), 3(3), 4(1) or (8), 5(3), 6(6), 9(4)[^{F37}, [^{F38}15(7), 15A(8) or 15B(7)]]—

    (a)   a Minister of the Crown,

    (b)   a person or body listed in Part 1 of Schedule 1, and

    (c)   a person or body listed in Part 3 of Schedule 1.

(2) In proceedings under subsection (1) the High Court or the Court of Session may grant any relief, or make any order, that it thinks appropriate.

[^{F39}(3) In relation to emergencies that do not fall within section 1(1)(c), the power under subsection (1)(a) to bring proceedings in respect of a failure by the Chief Constable (PSNI) is exercisable by the Department of Justice in Northern Ireland (and not by a Minister of the Crown).]

Changes to legislation: Civil Contingencies Act 2004 is up to date with all changes known to be in force on or before 21 August 2022. There are changes that may be brought into force at a future date. Changes that have been made appear in the content and are referenced with annotations. (See end of Document for details) View outstanding changes

Textual Amendments

F37   Words in s. 10(1) substituted (12.4.2010) by The Northern Ireland Act 1998 (Devolution of Policing and Justice Functions) Order 2010 (S.I. 2010/976), arts. 1(2), 5, **Sch. 3 para. 102(2)** (with arts. 28-31, Sch. 3 para. 110)

F38   Words in s. 10(1) substituted (24.5.2018) by The Welsh Ministers (Transfer of Functions) Order 2018 (S.I. 2018/644), arts. 1(1), **41(9)**

F39   S. 10(3) inserted (12.4.2010) by The Northern Ireland Act 1998 (Devolution of Policing and Justice Functions) Order 2010 (S.I. 2010/976), arts. 1(2), 5, **Sch. 3 para. 102(3)** (with arts. 28-31, Sch. 3 para. 110)

11   **Enforcement: Scotland**

(1) Any of the following may bring proceedings in the Court of Session in respect of a failure by a person or body listed in Part 2 or 4 of Schedule 1 to comply with section 2(1), 3(3), 4(1) or (8), 5(3), 6(6), 9(4) or 15(7)—

    (a)   the Scottish Ministers,

    (b)   a person or body listed in Part 2 of Schedule 1, and

    (c)   a person or body listed in Part 4 of Schedule 1.

(2) In proceedings under subsection (1) the Court of Session may grant any remedy, or make any order, that it thinks appropriate.

Modifications etc. (not altering text)

C2   S. 11 partly in force; s. 11 not in force at Royal Assent see s. 34; s. 11 in force (S.) at. 14.11.2005 by S.S.I. 2005/493, **art. 4**

[F40 11A. Enforcement: Wales

(1) Any of the following may bring proceedings in the High Court in respect of a failure by a person or body listed in Part 2A or 5 of Schedule 1 to comply with section 2(1), 3(3), 4(1) or (8), 5(3), 6(6), 9(4) or 15B(7)—

    (a)   the Welsh Ministers,

    (b)   a person or body listed in Part 2A of Schedule 1, and

    (c)   a person or body listed in Part 5 of Schedule 1.

(2) In proceedings under subsection (1) the High Court may grant any relief, or make any order, that it thinks appropriate.]

Textual Amendments

F40   S. 11A inserted (24.5.2018) by The Welsh Ministers (Transfer of Functions) Order 2018 (S.I. 2018/644), arts. 1(1), **41(10)**

12   **Provision of information**

Regulations or an order under this Part may, if addressing the provision or disclosure of information, make provision about—

16

Civil Contingencies Act 2004 (c. 36)
Part 1 – Local Arrangements for Civil Protection
Document Generated: 2022-08-21

Changes to legislation: Civil Contingencies Act 2004 is up to date with all changes known to be in force on or before
21 August 2022. There are changes that may be brought into force at a future date. Changes that have been made
appear in the content and are referenced with annotations. (See end of Document for details) View outstanding changes

    (a)   timing;

    (b)   the form in which information is provided;

    (c)   the use to which information may be put;

    (d)   storage of information;

    (e)   disposal of information.

[F41 12A Northern Ireland: provision or disclosure of national security information

(1) A Minister of the Crown may, for the purposes mentioned in subsection (2), make regulations addressing the provision or disclosure of national security information.

(2) Regulations under this section are to apply for the purposes of any regulations or order made by the Department of Justice in Northern Ireland under this Part; and any regulations or order made by the Department has effect subject to regulations under this section.

(3) "National security information" means information the disclosure of which to the public would, or would be likely to, adversely affect national security.

(4) Regulations under this section may (in particular)—

    (a)   provide that national security information is not to be provided or disclosed, or is to be provided or disclosed only in specified circumstances or in a specified way, despite any provision of regulations or an order made by the Department of Justice;

    (b)   provide that a certificate signed by a Minister of the Crown certifying that the disclosure of information to the public would, or would be likely to, adversely affect national security is conclusive evidence of that fact;

    (c)   provide that such a certificate may identify the information to which it applies by means of a general description and may be expressed to apply to information within that description that comes into existence after the certificate is made;

    (d)   confer other functions on a Minister of the Crown or any other specified person or body (and a function conferred may, in particular, be a power or duty to exercise a discretion).]

Textual Amendments

F41 S. 12A inserted (12.4.2010) by The Northern Ireland Act 1998 (Devolution of Policing and Justice Functions) Order 2010 (S.I. 2010/976), arts. 1(2), 5, **Sch. 3 para. 103** (with arts. 28-31, Sch. 3 para. 110)

13   Amendment of lists of responders

(1) A Minister of the Crown may by order amend Schedule 1 so as to—

    (a)   add an entry to Part 1 or 3;

    (b)   remove an entry from Part 1 or 3;

    (c)   move an entry from Part 1 to Part 3 or vice versa.

(2) The Scottish Ministers may by order amend Schedule 1 so as to—

    (a)   add an entry to Part 2 or 4;

    (b)   remove an entry from Part 2 or 4;

Changes to legislation: Civil Contingencies Act 2004 is up to date with all changes known to be in force on or before 21 August 2022. There are changes that may be brought into force at a future date. Changes that have been made appear in the content and are referenced with annotations. (See end of Document for details) View outstanding changes

(c) move an entry from Part 2 to Part 4 or vice versa.

[**F42**(2A) The Welsh Ministers may by order amend Schedule 1 so as to—

(a) add an entry for a devolved Welsh authority to Part 2A or 5;

(b) remove an entry from Part 2A or 5;

(c) move an entry from Part 2A to Part 5 or vice versa.

(2B) In subsection (2A) "devolved Welsh authority" has the meaning given in section 157A of the Government of Wales Act 2006.]

(3) An order under [**F43**subsection (1), (2) or (2A)] —

(a) may add, remove or move an entry either generally or only in relation to specified functions of a person or body, and

(b) may make incidental, transitional or consequential provision (which may include provision amending this Act or another enactment).

[**F44**(4) In relation to emergencies that do not fall within section 1(1)(c), the power under subsection (1) to make provision in relation to the Chief Constable (PSNI) is exercisable by the Department of Justice in Northern Ireland (and not by a Minister of the Crown).]

Textual Amendments

F42 S. 13(2A)(2B) inserted (24.5.2018) by The Welsh Ministers (Transfer of Functions) Order 2018 (S.I. 2018/644), arts. 1(1), **41(11)(a)**

F43 Words in s. 13(3) substituted (24.5.2018) by The Welsh Ministers (Transfer of Functions) Order 2018 (S.I. 2018/644), arts. 1(1), **41(11)(b)**

F44 S. 13(4) inserted (12.4.2010) by The Northern Ireland Act 1998 (Devolution of Policing and Justice Functions) Order 2010 (S.I. 2010/976), arts. 1(2), 5, **Sch. 3 para. 104(2)** (with arts. 28-31, Sch. 3 para. 110)

Commencement Information

I8 S. 13 partly in force; s. 13 not in force at Royal Assent see s. 34; s. 13(1)(3) in force for specified purposes at 22.7.2005 by S.I. 2005/2040, **art. 2(e)**; s. 13(2) in force and s. 13(3) in force for specified purposes (S.) at 6.10.2005 by S.S.I. 2005/493, **art. 3(i)(j)**

14 Scotland: consultation

(1) A Minister of the Crown shall consult the Scottish Ministers before making regulations or an order under this Part in relation to a person or body if or in so far as the person or body exercises functions in relation to Scotland.

(2) The Scottish Ministers shall consult a Minister of the Crown before making regulations or an order under this Part.

Commencement Information

I9 S. 14 partly in force; s. 14 not in force at Royal Assent see s. 34; s. 14(1) in force at 14.11.2005 by S.I. 2005/2040, **art. 3(j)**; s. 14(2) in force (S.) at 6.10.2005 by S.S.I. 2005/493, **art. 3(k)**

18

Civil Contingencies Act 2004 (c. 36)
Part 1 – Local Arrangements for Civil Protection
Document Generated: 2022-08-21

Changes to legislation: *Civil Contingencies Act 2004 is up to date with all changes known to be in force on or before 21 August 2022. There are changes that may be brought into force at a future date. Changes that have been made appear in the content and are referenced with annotations. (See end of Document for details) View outstanding changes*

[F45 14A Northern Ireland: consultation

(1) A Minister of the Crown must consult the Department of Justice in Northern Ireland before making regulations or an order under this Part in relation to the Chief Constable (PSNI).

(2) The Department of Justice must consult a Minister of the Crown before making regulations or an order under this Part.]

Textual Amendments

F45 S. 14A inserted (12.4.2010) by The Northern Ireland Act 1998 (Devolution of Policing and Justice Functions) Order 2010 (S.I. 2010/976), arts. 1(2), 5, **Sch. 3 para. 105** (with arts. 28-31, Sch. 3 para. 110)

[F46 14B. Wales: consultation

(1) A Minister of the Crown must consult the Welsh Ministers before making regulations or an order under this Part in relation to a person or body if or in so far as the person or body exercises functions in relation to Wales.

(2) The Welsh Ministers must consult a Minister of the Crown before making regulations or an order under this Part.]

Textual Amendments

F46 S. 14B inserted (24.5.2018) by The Welsh Ministers (Transfer of Functions) Order 2018 (S.I. 2018/644), arts. 1(1), **41(12)**

15   Scotland: cross-border collaboration

(1) Where a person or body listed in [F47 Part 1 or 2A] of Schedule 1 has a duty under section 2 or 4, the Scottish Ministers may make regulations—

    (a) permitting or requiring a person or body listed in Part 2 or 4 of that Schedule to co-operate, to such extent and in such manner as may be specified, with the person or body listed in [F47 Part 1 or 2A] of that Schedule in connection with the performance of the duty;

    (b) permitting or requiring a person or body listed in Part 2 or 4 of that Schedule to provide information, either on request or in other specified circumstances, to the person or body listed in [F47 Part 1 or 2A] of that Schedule in connection with the performance of the duty.

(2) The Scottish Ministers may issue guidance about a matter addressed in regulations under subsection (1).

(3) Where a person or body listed in Part 2 of Schedule 1 has a duty under section 2 or 4, a Minister of the Crown may make regulations—

    (a) permitting or requiring a person or body listed in Part 1 or 3 of that Schedule to co-operate, to such extent and in such manner as may be specified, with the person or body listed in Part 2 of that Schedule in connection with the performance of the duty;

Changes to legislation: Civil Contingencies Act 2004 is up to date with all changes known to be in force on or before 21 August 2022. There are changes that may be brought into force at a future date. Changes that have been made appear in the content and are referenced with annotations. (See end of Document for details) View outstanding changes

(b)   permitting or requiring a person or body listed in Part 1 or 3 of that Schedule to provide information, either on request or in other specified circumstances, to the person or body listed in Part 2 of that Schedule in connection with the performance of the duty.

(4) A Minister of the Crown may issue guidance about a matter addressed in regulations under subsection (3).

(5) If [^{F48}an order is made] under [^{F49}section 5(1) or (2A)] imposing a duty on a person or body listed in [^{F50}Part 1 or 2A] of Schedule 1, the Scottish Ministers may make an order—

(a)   permitting or requiring a person or body listed in Part 2 or 4 of that Schedule to co-operate, to such extent and in such manner as may be specified, with the person or body listed in [^{F50}Part 1 or 2A] of that Schedule in connection with the duty;

(b)   permitting or requiring a person or body listed in Part 2 or 4 of that Schedule to provide information, either on request or in other specified circumstances, to the person or body listed in [^{F50}Part 1 or 2A] of that Schedule in connection with the duty.

(6) If the Scottish Ministers make an order under section 5(2) imposing a duty on a person or body listed in Part 2 of Schedule 1, a Minister of the Crown may make an order—

(a)   permitting or requiring a person or body listed in Part 1 or 3 of that Schedule to co-operate, to such extent and in such manner as may be specified, with the person or body listed in Part 2 of that Schedule in connection with the duty;

(b)   permitting or requiring a person or body listed in Part 1 or 3 of that Schedule to provide information, either on request or in other specified circumstances, to the person or body listed in Part 2 of that Schedule in connection with the duty.

(7) A person or body shall—

(a)   comply with regulations or an order under this section, and

(b)   have regard to guidance under this section.

(8) In this Act, except where the contrary intention appears—

(a)   a reference to an order under section 5(1) includes a reference to an order under subsection (6) above, and

(b)   a reference to an order under section 5(2) includes a reference to an order under subsection (5) above.

Textual Amendments

F47   Words in s. 15(1) substituted (24.5.2018) by The Welsh Ministers (Transfer of Functions) Order 2018 (S.I. 2018/644), arts. 1(1), **41(13)(a)**

F48   Words in s. 15(5) substituted (12.4.2010) by The Northern Ireland Act 1998 (Devolution of Policing and Justice Functions) Order 2010 (S.I. 2010/976), arts. 1(2), 5, **Sch. 3 para. 106(2)** (with arts. 28-31, Sch. 3 para. 110)

F49   Words in s. 15(5) substituted (24.5.2018) by The Welsh Ministers (Transfer of Functions) Order 2018 (S.I. 2018/644), arts. 1(1), **41(13)(b)(i)**

F50   Words in s. 15(5) substituted (24.5.2018) by The Welsh Ministers (Transfer of Functions) Order 2018 (S.I. 2018/644), arts. 1(1), **41(13)(b)(ii)**

20

Civil Contingencies Act 2004 (c. 36)
Part 1 – Local Arrangements for Civil Protection
Document Generated: 2022-08-21

Changes to legislation: *Civil Contingencies Act 2004 is up to date with all changes known to be in force on or before 21 August 2022. There are changes that may be brought into force at a future date. Changes that have been made appear in the content and are referenced with annotations. (See end of Document for details) View outstanding changes*

[F51]15A **Northern Ireland: cross-border collaboration**

(1) In relation to emergencies that do not fall within section 1(1)(c)—

    (a) the power under [F52section 15(3) or (6), or section 15B(3) or (6)] to make regulations or an order permitting or requiring the Chief Constable (PSNI) to co-operate with, or provide information to, a person or body listed in [F53Part 2 or 2A] of Schedule 1 is exercisable by the Department of Justice in Northern Ireland (and not by a Minister of the Crown);

    (b) the power under [F54section 15(4) or 15B(4)] to issue guidance is exercisable by the Department of Justice (and not by a Minister of the Crown) in relation to regulations made by the Department.

(2) Where the Chief Constable (PSNI) has a duty under section 2, a Minister of the Crown may, in relation to emergencies that do not fall within section 1(1)(c), make regulations—

    (a) permitting or requiring another person or body listed in Part 1 or 3 of Schedule 1 to co-operate, to such extent and in such manner as may be specified, with the Chief Constable (PSNI) in connection with the performance of the duty;

    (b) permitting or requiring another person or body listed in Part 1 or 3 of Schedule 1 to provide information, either on request or in other specified circumstances, to the Chief Constable (PSNI) in connection with the performance of the duty.

(3) A Minister of the Crown may issue guidance about a matter addressed in regulations under subsection (2).

(4) If the Department of Justice in Northern Ireland makes an order under section 5(1) imposing a duty on the Chief Constable (PSNI), a Minister of the Crown may make an order—

    (a) permitting or requiring another person or body listed in Part 1 or 3 of Schedule 1 to co-operate, to such extent and in such manner as may be specified, with the Chief Constable (PSNI) in connection with the duty;

    (b) permitting or requiring another person or body listed in Part 1 or 3 of Schedule 1 to provide information, either on request or in other specified circumstances, to the Chief Constable (PSNI) in connection with the duty.

(5) Where a person or body listed in Part 1 of Schedule 1 (other than the Chief Constable (PSNI)) has a duty under section 2 or 4, the Department of Justice in Northern Ireland may, in relation to emergencies that do not fall within section 1(1)(c), make regulations—

    (a) permitting or requiring the Chief Constable (PSNI) (if listed in Part 1 or 3 of Schedule 1) to co-operate, to such extent and in such manner as may be specified, with the person or body listed in Part 1 of Schedule 1 in connection with the performance of the duty;

    (b) permitting or requiring the Chief Constable (PSNI) (if listed in Part 1 or 3 of Schedule 1) to provide information, either on request or in other specified circumstances, to the person or body listed in Part 1 of Schedule 1 in connection with the performance of the duty.

(6) The Department of Justice in Northern Ireland may issue guidance about a matter addressed in regulations under subsection (5).

Changes to legislation: Civil Contingencies Act 2004 is up to date with all changes known to be in force on or before
21 August 2022. There are changes that may be brought into force at a future date. Changes that have been made
appear in the content and are referenced with annotations. (See end of Document for details) View outstanding changes

(7) If a Minister of the Crown makes an order under section 5(1) imposing a duty on a person or body listed in Part 1 of Schedule 1, the Department of Justice in Northern Ireland may, in relation to emergencies that do not fall within section 1(1)(c), make an order—

    (a) permitting or requiring the Chief Constable (PSNI) (if listed in Part 1 or 3 of Schedule 1) to co-operate, to such extent and in such manner as may be specified, with the person or body listed in Part 1 of Schedule 1 in connection with the duty;

    (b) permitting or requiring the Chief Constable (PSNI) (if listed in Part 1 or 3 of Schedule 1) to provide information, either on request or in other specified circumstances, to the person or body listed in Part 1 of Schedule 1 in connection with the duty.

(8) A person or body must comply with regulations or an order under this section and must have regard to guidance under this section.

(9) In this Act, except where the contrary intention appears, a reference to an order under section 5(1) includes a reference to an order under subsection (4) or (7) above.]

Textual Amendments

F51 S. 15A inserted (12.4.2010) by The Northern Ireland Act 1998 (Devolution of Policing and Justice Functions) Order 2010 (S.I. 2010/976), arts. 1(2), 5, **Sch. 3 para. 107** (with arts. 28-31, Sch. 3 para. 110)

F52 Words in s. 15A(1)(a) substituted (24.5.2018) by The Welsh Ministers (Transfer of Functions) Order 2018 (S.I. 2018/644), arts. 1(1), **41(14)(a)(i)**

F53 Words in s. 15A(1)(a) substituted (24.5.2018) by The Welsh Ministers (Transfer of Functions) Order 2018 (S.I. 2018/644), arts. 1(1), **41(14)(a)(ii)**

F54 Words in s. 15A(1)(b) substituted (24.5.2018) by The Welsh Ministers (Transfer of Functions) Order 2018 (S.I. 2018/644), arts. 1(1), **41(14)(b)**

[F55 15B. Wales: cross-border collaboration

(1) Where a person or body listed in Part 1 or 2 of Schedule 1 has a duty under section 2 or 4, the Welsh Ministers may make regulations—

    (a) permitting or requiring a person or body listed in Part 2A or 5 of that Schedule to co-operate, to such extent and in such manner as may be specified, with the person or body listed in Part 1 or 2 of that Schedule in connection with the performance of the duty;

    (b) permitting or requiring a person or body listed in Part 2A or 5 of that Schedule to provide information, either on request or in other specified circumstances, to the person or body listed in Part 1 or 2 of that Schedule in connection with the performance of the duty.

(2) The Welsh Ministers may issue guidance about a matter addressed in regulations under subsection (1).

(3) Where a person or body listed in Part 2A of Schedule 1 has a duty under section 2 or 4, a Minister of the Crown may make regulations—

    (a) permitting or requiring a person or body listed in Part 1 or 3 of that Schedule to co-operate, to such extent and in such manner as may be specified, with

22

Civil Contingencies Act 2004 (c. 36)
Part 1 – Local Arrangements for Civil Protection
Document Generated: 2022-08-21

the person or body listed in Part 2A of that Schedule in connection with the performance of the duty;

(b) permitting or requiring a person or body listed in Part 1 or 3 of that Schedule to provide information, either on request or in other specified circumstances, to the person or body listed in Part 2A of that Schedule in connection with the performance of the duty.

(4) A Minister of the Crown may issue guidance about a matter addressed in regulations under subsection (3).

(5) If an order is made under section 5(1) or (2) imposing a duty on a person or body listed in Part 1 or 2 of Schedule 1, the Welsh Ministers may make an order—

(a) permitting or requiring a person or body listed in Part 2A or 5 of that Schedule to co-operate, to such extent and in such manner as may be specified, with the person or body listed in Part 1 or 2 of that Schedule in connection with the duty;

(b) permitting or requiring a person or body listed in Part 2A or 5 of that Schedule to provide information, either on request or in other specified circumstances, to the person or body listed in Part 1 or 2 of that Schedule in connection with the duty.

(6) If the Welsh Ministers make an order under section 5(2A) imposing a duty on a person or body listed in Part 2A of Schedule 1, a Minister of the Crown may make an order—

(a) permitting or requiring a person or body listed in Part 1 or 3 of that Schedule to co-operate, to such extent and in such manner as may be specified, with the person or body listed in Part 2A of that Schedule in connection with the duty;

(b) permitting or requiring a person or body listed in Part 1 or 3 of that Schedule to provide information, either on request or in other specified circumstances, to the person or body listed in Part 2A of that Schedule in connection with the duty.

(7) A person or body must—

(a) comply with regulations or an order under this section, and

(b) have regard to guidance under this section.

(8) In this Act, except where the contrary intention appears—

(a) a reference to an order under section 5(1) includes a reference to an order under subsection (6) above; and

(b) a reference to an order under section 5(2A) includes a reference to an order under subsection (5) above.]

Textual Amendments

F55 S. 15B inserted (24.5.2018) by The Welsh Ministers (Transfer of Functions) Order 2018 (S.I. 2018/644), arts. 1(1), **41(15)**

16   National Assembly for Wales

[F56](1) . . . .

Changes to legislation: *Civil Contingencies Act 2004 is up to date with all changes known to be in force on or before 21 August 2022. There are changes that may be brought into force at a future date. Changes that have been made appear in the content and are referenced with annotations. (See end of Document for details) View outstanding changes*

---

(2) A Minister of the Crown may not without the consent of the National Assembly for Wales take action of a kind specified in subsection (3) that relates wholly or partly to a person or body specified in subsection (4).

(3) The actions referred to in subsection (2) are—

   (a) making regulations under section 2(3), 4(2) or 6(1),

   (b) making an order under section 5(1),

   (c) issuing guidance under section 3(1), 4(6) or 6(4),

   (d) giving a direction under section 7,

   (e) bringing proceedings under section 10, and

   (f) making an order under section 13.

(4) The persons and bodies referred to in subsection (2) are—

   [F57](a) . . . .

   (b) a person or body specified in [F58paragraph 9 or 10 of Schedule 1], if and in so far as the person or body has functions in relation to Wales.

Textual Amendments

F56 S. 16(1) omitted (24.5.2018) by virtue of The Welsh Ministers (Transfer of Functions) Order 2018 (S.I. 2018/644), arts. 1(1), **41(16)(a)**

F57 S. 16(4)(a) omitted (24.5.2018) by virtue of The Welsh Ministers (Transfer of Functions) Order 2018 (S.I. 2018/644), arts. 1(1), **41(16)(b)**

F58 Words in s. 16(4)(b) substituted (24.5.2018) by The Welsh Ministers (Transfer of Functions) Order 2018 (S.I. 2018/644), arts. 1(1), **41(16)(c)**

17 Regulations and orders

(1) Regulations and orders under this Part shall be made [F59by a Minister of the Crown [F60, the Scottish Ministers or the Welsh Ministers]] by statutory instrument.

[F61(1A) Any power of the Department of Justice in Northern Ireland under this Part to make regulations or an order is exercisable by statutory rule for the purposes of the M1Statutory Rules (Northern Ireland) Order 1979.]

(2) An order under section 1(4), 5(1) or 13(1) may not be made by a Minister of the Crown unless a draft has been laid before and approved by resolution of each House of Parliament.

(3) An order under section 1(4), 5(2) or 13(2) may not be made by the Scottish Ministers unless a draft has been laid before and approved by resolution of the Scottish Parliament.

[F62(3ZA) An order under section 5(2A) or 13(2A) may not be made by the Welsh Ministers unless a draft has been laid before and approved by a resolution of the National Assembly for Wales.]

[F63(3A) An order under section 1(4), 5(1) or 13(1) may not be made by the Department of Justice in Northern Ireland unless a draft has been laid before and approved by resolution of the Northern Ireland Assembly.

24

Civil Contingencies Act 2004 (c. 36)
Part 1 – Local Arrangements for Civil Protection
Document Generated: 2022-08-21

Changes to legislation: *Civil Contingencies Act 2004 is up to date with all changes known to be in force on or before 21 August 2022. There are changes that may be brought into force at a future date. Changes that have been made appear in the content and are referenced with annotations. (See end of Document for details) View outstanding changes*

(3B) Section 41(3) of the Interpretation Act (Northern Ireland) 1954 applies for the purposes of subsection (3A) in relation to the laying of a draft as it applies in relation to the laying of a statutory document under an enactment.]

(4) Regulations made by a Minister of the Crown under this Part shall be subject to annulment in pursuance of a resolution of either House of Parliament.

(5) Regulations made by the Scottish Ministers under this Part shall be subject to annulment in pursuance of a resolution of the Scottish Parliament.

[F64(5ZA) Regulations made by the Welsh Ministers under this Part are subject to annulment in pursuance of a resolution of the National Assembly for Wales.]

[F65(5A) Regulations made by the Department of Justice in Northern Ireland under this Part are subject to negative resolution (within the meaning of section 41(6) of the Interpretation Act (Northern Ireland) 1954).]

(6) Regulations or an order under this Part—

    (a)   may make provision which applies generally or only in specified circumstances or for a specified purpose,

    (b)   may make different provision for different circumstances or purposes, and

    (c)   may make incidental, consequential or transitional provision.

Textual Amendments

F59   Words in s. 17(1) inserted (12.4.2010) by The Northern Ireland Act 1998 (Devolution of Policing and Justice Functions) Order 2010 (S.I. 2010/976), arts. 1(2), 5, **Sch. 3 para. 108(2)** (with arts. 28-31, Sch. 3 para. 110)

F60   Words in s. 17(1) substituted (24.5.2018) by The Welsh Ministers (Transfer of Functions) Order 2018 (S.I. 2018/644), arts. 1(1), **41(17)(a)**

F61   S. 17(1A) inserted (12.4.2010) by The Northern Ireland Act 1998 (Devolution of Policing and Justice Functions) Order 2010 (S.I. 2010/976), arts. 1(2), 5, **Sch. 3 para. 108(3)** (with arts. 28-31, Sch. 3 para. 110)

F62   S. 17(3ZA) inserted (24.5.2018) by The Welsh Ministers (Transfer of Functions) Order 2018 (S.I. 2018/644), arts. 1(1), **41(17)(b)**

F63   S. 17(3A)(3B) inserted (12.4.2010) by The Northern Ireland Act 1998 (Devolution of Policing and Justice Functions) Order 2010 (S.I. 2010/976), arts. 1(2), 5, **Sch. 3 para. 108(4)** (with arts. 28-31, Sch. 3 para. 110)

F64   S. 17(5ZA) inserted (24.5.2018) by The Welsh Ministers (Transfer of Functions) Order 2018 (S.I. 2018/644), arts. 1(1), **41(17)(c)**

F65   S. 17(5A) inserted (12.4.2010) by The Northern Ireland Act 1998 (Devolution of Policing and Justice Functions) Order 2010 (S.I. 2010/976), arts. 1(2), 5, **Sch. 3 para. 108(5)** (with arts. 28-31, Sch. 3 para. 110)

Commencement Information

I10   S. 17 partly in force; s. 17 not in force at Royal Assent see s. 34; s. 17(6) in force for specified purposes at 22.7.2005 and s. 17(1)(2)(4) in force for specified purposes at 14.11.2005 by S.I. 2005/2040, **arts. 2(g), 3(l)**; s. 17(3)(5) in force and s. 17(1)(6) in force for specified purposes (S.) at 6.10.2005 by S.S.I. 2005/493, **art. 3(l)(m)**

Marginal Citations

M1   S.I. 1979/1573 (N.I. 12).

Changes to legislation: Civil Contingencies Act 2004 is up to date with all changes known to be in force on or before
21 August 2022. There are changes that may be brought into force at a future date. Changes that have been made
appear in the content and are referenced with annotations. (See end of Document for details) View outstanding changes

18 Interpretation, &c.

(1) In this Part—

"enactment" includes—

(a) an Act of the Scottish Parliament,

(b) Northern Ireland legislation, and

(c) an instrument made under an Act of the Scottish Parliament or under Northern Ireland legislation (as well as an instrument made under an Act),

[F66"Chief Constable (PSNI)" means the Chief Constable of the Police Service of Northern Ireland,]

"function" means any power or duty whether conferred by virtue of an enactment or otherwise,

"terrorism" has the meaning given by section 1 of the Terrorism Act 2000 (c. 11), and

"war" includes armed conflict.

(2) In this Part a reference to the United Kingdom includes a reference to the territorial sea of the United Kingdom.

(3) Except in a case of contradiction, nothing in or done under this Part shall impliedly repeal or revoke a provision of or made under another enactment.

Textual Amendments

F66 Words in s. 18(1) inserted (12.4.2010) by The Northern Ireland Act 1998 (Devolution of Policing and Justice Functions) Order 2010 (S.I. 2010/976), arts. 1(2), 5, **Sch. 3 para. 109** (with arts. 28-31, Sch. 3 para. 110)

PART 2

EMERGENCY POWERS

19 Meaning of "emergency"

(1) In this Part "emergency" means—

(a) an event or situation which threatens serious damage to human welfare in the United Kingdom or in a Part or region,

(b) an event or situation which threatens serious damage to the environment of the United Kingdom or of a Part or region, or

(c) war, or terrorism, which threatens serious damage to the security of the United Kingdom.

(2) For the purposes of subsection (1)(a) an event or situation threatens damage to human welfare only if it involves, causes or may cause—

(a) loss of human life,

(b) human illness or injury,

(c) homelessness,

(d) damage to property,

Changes to legislation: Civil Contingencies Act 2004 is up to date with all changes known to be in force on or before
21 August 2022. There are changes that may be brought into force at a future date. Changes that have been made
appear in the content and are referenced with annotations. (See end of Document for details) View outstanding changes

   (e)   disruption of a supply of money, food, water, energy or fuel,

   (f)   disruption of a system of communication,

   (g)   disruption of facilities for transport, or

   (h)   disruption of services relating to health.

(3) For the purposes of subsection (1)(b) an event or situation threatens damage to the environment only if it involves, causes or may cause—

   (a)   contamination of land, water or air with biological, chemical or radio-active matter, or

   (b)   disruption or destruction of plant life or animal life.

(4) The Secretary of State may by order amend subsection (2) so as to provide that in so far as an event or situation involves or causes disruption of a specified supply, system, facility or service—

   (a)   it is to be treated as threatening damage to human welfare, or

   (b)   it is no longer to be treated as threatening damage to human welfare.

(5) An order under subsection (4)—

   (a)   may make consequential amendment of this Part, and

   (b)   may not be made unless a draft has been laid before, and approved by resolution of, each House of Parliament.

(6) The event or situation mentioned in subsection (1) may occur or be inside or outside the United Kingdom.

20   Power to make emergency regulations

(1) Her Majesty may by Order in Council make emergency regulations if satisfied that the conditions in section 21 are satisfied.

(2) A senior Minister of the Crown may make emergency regulations if satisfied—

   (a)   that the conditions in section 21 are satisfied, and

   (b)   that it would not be possible, without serious delay, to arrange for an Order in Council under subsection (1).

(3) In this Part "senior Minister of the Crown" means—

   (a)   the First Lord of the Treasury (the Prime Minister),

   (b)   any of Her Majesty's Principal Secretaries of State, and

   (c)   the Commissioners of Her Majesty's Treasury.

(4) In this Part "serious delay" means a delay that might—

   (a)   cause serious damage, or

   (b)   seriously obstruct the prevention, control or mitigation of serious damage.

(5) Regulations under this section must be prefaced by a statement by the person making the regulations—

   (a)   specifying the nature of the emergency in respect of which the regulations are made, and

   (b)   declaring that the person making the regulations—

       (i)   is satisfied that the conditions in section 21 are met,

       (ii)   is satisfied that the regulations contain only provision which is appropriate for the purpose of preventing, controlling or mitigating an

Changes to legislation: Civil Contingencies Act 2004 is up to date with all changes known to be in force on or before 21 August 2022. There are changes that may be brought into force at a future date. Changes that have been made appear in the content and are referenced with annotations. (See end of Document for details) View outstanding changes

> aspect or effect of the emergency in respect of which the regulations are made,
> (iii) is satisfied that the effect of the regulations is in due proportion to that aspect or effect of the emergency,
> (iv) is satisfied that the regulations are compatible with the Convention rights (within the meaning of section 1 of the Human Rights Act 1998 (c. 42)), and
> (v) in the case of regulations made under subsection (2), is satisfied as to the matter specified in subsection (2)(b).

21 Conditions for making emergency regulations

(1) This section specifies the conditions mentioned in section 20.

(2) The first condition is that an emergency has occurred, is occurring or is about to occur.

(3) The second condition is that it is necessary to make provision for the purpose of preventing, controlling or mitigating an aspect or effect of the emergency.

(4) The third condition is that the need for provision referred to in subsection (3) is urgent.

(5) For the purpose of subsection (3) provision which is the same as an enactment ("the existing legislation") is necessary if, in particular—
  (a) the existing legislation cannot be relied upon without the risk of serious delay,
  (b) it is not possible without the risk of serious delay to ascertain whether the existing legislation can be relied upon, or
  (c) the existing legislation might be insufficiently effective.

(6) For the purpose of subsection (3) provision which could be made under an enactment other than section 20 ("the existing legislation") is necessary if, in particular—
  (a) the provision cannot be made under the existing legislation without the risk of serious delay,
  (b) it is not possible without the risk of serious delay to ascertain whether the provision can be made under the existing legislation, or
  (c) the provision might be insufficiently effective if made under the existing legislation.

22 Scope of emergency regulations

(1) Emergency regulations may make any provision which the person making the regulations is satisfied is appropriate for the purpose of preventing, controlling or mitigating an aspect or effect of the emergency in respect of which the regulations are made.

(2) In particular, emergency regulations may make any provision which the person making the regulations is satisfied is appropriate for the purpose of—
  (a) protecting human life, health or safety,
  (b) treating human illness or injury,
  (c) protecting or restoring property,
  (d) protecting or restoring a supply of money, food, water, energy or fuel,
  (e) protecting or restoring a system of communication,
  (f) protecting or restoring facilities for transport,

Changes to legislation: *Civil Contingencies Act 2004 is up to date with all changes known to be in force on or before 21 August 2022. There are changes that may be brought into force at a future date. Changes that have been made appear in the content and are referenced with annotations. (See end of Document for details) View outstanding changes*

(g)   protecting or restoring the provision of services relating to health,

(h)   protecting or restoring the activities of banks or other financial institutions,

(i)   preventing, containing or reducing the contamination of land, water or air,

(j)   preventing, reducing or mitigating the effects of disruption or destruction of plant life or animal life,

(k)   protecting or restoring activities of Parliament, of the Scottish Parliament, of the Northern Ireland Assembly or of the National Assembly for Wales, or

(l)   protecting or restoring the performance of public functions.

(3) Emergency regulations may make provision of any kind that could be made by Act of Parliament or by the exercise of the Royal Prerogative; in particular, regulations may—

(a)   confer a function on a Minister of the Crown, on the Scottish Ministers, on the National Assembly for Wales, on a Northern Ireland department, on a coordinator appointed under section 24 or on any other specified person (and a function conferred may, in particular, be—

(i) a power, or duty, to exercise a discretion;

(ii) a power to give directions or orders, whether written or oral);

(b)   provide for or enable the requisition or confiscation of property (with or without compensation);

(c)   provide for or enable the destruction of property, animal life or plant life (with or without compensation);

(d)   prohibit, or enable the prohibition of, movement to or from a specified place;

(e)   require, or enable the requirement of, movement to or from a specified place;

(f)   prohibit, or enable the prohibition of, assemblies of specified kinds, at specified places or at specified times;

(g)   prohibit, or enable the prohibition of, travel at specified times;

(h)   prohibit, or enable the prohibition of, other specified activities;

(i)   create an offence of—

(i) failing to comply with a provision of the regulations;

(ii) failing to comply with a direction or order given or made under the regulations;

(iii) obstructing a person in the performance of a function under or by virtue of the regulations;

(j)   disapply or modify an enactment or a provision made under or by virtue of an enactment;

(k)   require a person or body to act in performance of a function (whether the function is conferred by the regulations or otherwise and whether or not the regulations also make provision for remuneration or compensation);

(l)   enable the Defence Council to authorise the deployment of Her Majesty's armed forces;

(m)   make provision (which may include conferring powers in relation to property) for facilitating any deployment of Her Majesty's armed forces;

(n)   confer jurisdiction on a court or tribunal (which may include a tribunal established by the regulations);

(o)   make provision which has effect in relation to, or to anything done in—

(i) an area of the territorial sea,

(ii) an area within British fishery limits, or

          (iii) an area of the continental shelf;

    (p) make provision which applies generally or only in specified circumstances or for a specified purpose;

    (q) make different provision for different circumstances or purposes.

(4) In subsection (3) "specified" means specified by, or to be specified in accordance with, the regulations.

(5) A person making emergency regulations must have regard to the importance of ensuring that Parliament, the High Court and the Court of Session are able to conduct proceedings in connection with—

    (a) the regulations, or

    (b) action taken under the regulations.

23 Limitations of emergency regulations

(1) Emergency regulations may make provision only if and in so far as the person making the regulations is satisfied—

    (a) that the provision is appropriate for the purpose of preventing, controlling or mitigating an aspect or effect of the emergency in respect of which the regulations are made, and

    (b) that the effect of the provision is in due proportion to that aspect or effect of the emergency.

(2) Emergency regulations must specify the Parts of the United Kingdom or regions in relation to which the regulations have effect.

(3) Emergency regulations may not—

    (a) require a person, or enable a person to be required, to provide military service, or

    (b) prohibit or enable the prohibition of participation in, or any activity in connection with, a strike or other industrial action.

(4) Emergency regulations may not—

    (a) create an offence other than one of the kind described in section 22(3)(i),

    (b) create an offence other than one which is triable only before a magistrates' court or, in Scotland, before a sheriff under summary procedure,

    (c) create an offence which is punishable—

        (i) with imprisonment for a period exceeding three months, or

        (ii) with a fine exceeding level 5 on the standard scale, or

    (d) alter procedure in relation to criminal proceedings.

(5) Emergency regulations may not amend—

    (a) this Part of this Act, or

    (b) the Human Rights Act 1998 (c. 42).

24 Regional and Emergency Coordinators

(1) Emergency regulations must require a senior Minister of the Crown to appoint—

*Changes to legislation: Civil Contingencies Act 2004 is up to date with all changes known to be in force on or before
21 August 2022. There are changes that may be brought into force at a future date. Changes that have been made
appear in the content and are referenced with annotations. (See end of Document for details) View outstanding changes*

(a)   for each Part of the United Kingdom, other than England, in relation to which the regulations have effect, a person to be known as the Emergency Coordinator for that Part, and

(b)   for each region in relation to which the regulations have effect, a person to be known as the Regional Nominated Coordinator for that region.

(2) Provision made in accordance with subsection (1) may, in particular, include provision about the coordinator's—

(a)   terms of appointment,

(b)   conditions of service (including remuneration), and

(c)   functions.

(3) The principal purpose of the appointment shall be to facilitate coordination of activities under the emergency regulations (whether only in the Part or region for which the appointment is made or partly there and partly elsewhere).

(4) In exercising his functions a coordinator shall—

(a)   comply with a direction of a senior Minister of the Crown, and

(b)   have regard to guidance issued by a senior Minister of the Crown.

(5) A coordinator shall not be regarded as the servant or agent of the Crown or as enjoying any status, immunity or privilege of the Crown.

[F67]25   Establishment of tribunal

. . . .

Textual Amendments

F67   S. 25 omitted (19.9.2013) by virtue of The Public Bodies (Abolition of Administrative Justice and Tribunals Council) Order 2013 (S.I. 2013/2042), art. 1(2), **Sch. para. 29**

26   Duration

(1) Emergency regulations shall lapse—

(a)   at the end of the period of 30 days beginning with the date on which they are made, or

(b)   at such earlier time as may be specified in the regulations.

(2) Subsection (1)—

(a)   shall not prevent the making of new regulations, and

(b)   shall not affect anything done by virtue of the regulations before they lapse.

27   Parliamentary scrutiny

(1) Where emergency regulations are made—

(a)   a senior Minister of the Crown shall as soon as is reasonably practicable lay the regulations before Parliament, and

(b)   the regulations shall lapse at the end of the period of seven days beginning with the date of laying unless during that period each House of Parliament passes a resolution approving them.

*Changes to legislation: Civil Contingencies Act 2004 is up to date with all changes known to be in force on or before
21 August 2022. There are changes that may be brought into force at a future date. Changes that have been made
appear in the content and are referenced with annotations. (See end of Document for details) View outstanding changes*

(2) If each House of Parliament passes a resolution that emergency regulations shall cease to have effect, the regulations shall cease to have effect—

    (a) at such time, after the passing of the resolutions, as may be specified in them, or

    (b) if no time is specified in the resolutions, at the beginning of the day after that on which the resolutions are passed (or, if they are passed on different days, at the beginning of the day after that on which the second resolution is passed).

(3) If each House of Parliament passes a resolution that emergency regulations shall have effect with a specified amendment, the regulations shall have effect as amended, with effect from—

    (a) such time, after the passing of the resolutions, as may be specified in them, or

    (b) if no time is specified in the resolutions, the beginning of the day after that on which the resolutions are passed (or, if they are passed on different days, the beginning of the day after that on which the second resolution is passed).

(4) Nothing in this section—

    (a) shall prevent the making of new regulations, or

    (b) shall affect anything done by virtue of regulations before they lapse, cease to have effect or are amended under this section.

28   Parliamentary scrutiny: prorogation and adjournment

(1) If when emergency regulations are made under section 20 Parliament stands prorogued to a day after the end of the period of five days beginning with the date on which the regulations are made, Her Majesty shall by proclamation under the Meeting of Parliament Act 1797 (c. 127) require Parliament to meet on a specified day within that period.

(2) If when emergency regulations are made under section 20 the House of Commons stands adjourned to a day after the end of the period of five days beginning with the date on which the regulations are made, the Speaker [F68of the House of Commons] shall arrange for the House to meet on a day during that period.

(3) If when emergency regulations are made under section 20 the House of Lords stands adjourned to a day after the end of the period of five days beginning with the date on which the regulations are made, [F69the Speaker of the House of Lords] shall arrange for the House to meet on a day during that period.

(4) In subsections (2) and (3) a reference to [F70the Speaker of the House of Commons or the Speaker of the House of Lords] includes a reference to a person authorised by Standing Orders of [F71the House of Commons or of the House of Lords] to act in place of [F70the Speaker of the House of Commons or the Speaker of the House of Lords] in respect of the recall of the House during adjournment.

Textual Amendments

F68   Words in s. 28(2) inserted (21.6.2006) by The Lord Chancellor (Transfer of Functions and Supplementary Provisions) (No. 3) Order 2006 (S.I. 2006/1640), arts. 1, 3, **Sch. 1 para. 1(2)**

F69   Words in s. 28(3) substituted (21.6.2006) by The Lord Chancellor (Transfer of Functions and Supplementary Provisions) (No. 3) Order 2006 (S.I. 2006/1640), arts. 1, 3, **Sch. 1 para. 1(3)**

Changes to legislation: Civil Contingencies Act 2004 is up to date with all changes known to be in force on or before 21 August 2022. There are changes that may be brought into force at a future date. Changes that have been made appear in the content and are referenced with annotations. (See end of Document for details) View outstanding changes

F70 Words in s. 28(4) substituted (21.6.2006) by The Lord Chancellor (Transfer of Functions and Supplementary Provisions) (No. 3) Order 2006 (S.I. 2006/1640), arts. 1, 3, **Sch. 1 para. 1(4)(a)**

F71 Words in s. 28(4) substitued (21.6.2006) by The Lord Chancellor (Transfer of Functions and Supplementary Provisions) (No. 3) Order 2006 (S.I. 2006/1640), arts. 1, 3, **Sch. 1 para. 1(4)(b)**

29 Consultation with devolved administrations

(1) Emergency regulations which relate wholly or partly to Scotland may not be made unless a senior Minister of the Crown has consulted the Scottish Ministers.

(2) Emergency regulations which relate wholly or partly to Northern Ireland may not be made unless a senior Minister of the Crown has consulted the First Minister and deputy First Minister.

(3) Emergency regulations which relate wholly or partly to Wales may not be made unless a senior Minister of the Crown has consulted the National Assembly for Wales.

(4) But—

    (a) a senior Minister of the Crown may disapply a requirement to consult if he thinks it necessary by reason of urgency, and

    (b) a failure to satisfy a requirement to consult shall not affect the validity of regulations.

30 Procedure

(1) Emergency regulations shall be made by statutory instrument (whether or not made by Order in Council).

(2) Emergency regulations shall be treated for the purposes of the Human Rights Act 1998 (c. 42) as subordinate legislation and not primary legislation (whether or not they amend primary legislation).

31 Interpretation

(1) In this Part—

    "British fishery limits" has the meaning given by the Fishery Limits Act 1976 (c. 86),

    "the continental shelf" means any area designated by Order in Council under section 1(7) of the Continental Shelf Act 1964 (c. 29),

    "emergency" has the meaning given by section 19,

    "enactment" includes—

    (a) an Act of the Scottish Parliament,

    (b) Northern Ireland legislation, and

    (c) an instrument made under an Act of the Scottish Parliament or under Northern Ireland legislation (as well as an instrument made under an Act),

    "function" means any power or duty whether conferred by virtue of an enactment or otherwise,

    "Part" in relation to the United Kingdom has the meaning given by subsection (2),

    "public functions" means—

33

Changes to legislation: Civil Contingencies Act 2004 is up to date with all changes known to be in force on or before
21 August 2022. There are changes that may be brought into force at a future date. Changes that have been made
appear in the content and are referenced with annotations. (See end of Document for details) View outstanding changes

    (a) functions conferred or imposed by or by virtue of an enactment,

    (b) functions of Ministers of the Crown (or their departments),

    (c) functions of persons holding office under the Crown,

    (d) functions of the Scottish Ministers,

    (e) functions of the Northern Ireland Ministers or of the Northern Ireland departments, and

    (f) functions of the National Assembly for Wales,

      "region" has the meaning given by subsection (2),

      "senior Minister of the Crown" has the meaning given by section 20(3),

      "serious delay" has the meaning given by section 20(4),

      "territorial sea" means the territorial sea adjacent to, or to any Part of, the United Kingdom, construed in accordance with section 1 of the Territorial Sea Act 1987 (c. 49),

      "terrorism" has the meaning given by section 1 of the Terrorism Act 2000 (c. 11), and

      "war" includes armed conflict.

(2) In this Part—

    (a) "Part" in relation to the United Kingdom means—

        (i) England,

        (ii) Northern Ireland,

        (iii) Scotland, and

        (iv) Wales,

    (b) "region" means a region for the purposes of the Regional Development Agencies Act 1998 (c. 45), and

    (c) a reference to a Part or region of the United Kingdom includes a reference to—

        (i) any part of the territorial sea that is adjacent to that Part or region,

        (ii) any part of the area within British fishery limits that is adjacent to the Part or region, and

        (iii) any part of the continental shelf that is adjacent to the Part or region.

(3) The following shall have effect for the purpose of subsection (2)—

    (a) an Order in Council under section 126(2) of the Scotland Act 1998 (c. 46) (apportionment of sea areas),

    (b) an Order in Council under section 98(8) of the Northern Ireland Act 1998 (c. 47) (apportionment of sea areas), and

    (c) an order under section 155(2) of the Government of Wales Act 1998 (c. 38) (apportionment of sea areas);

but only if or in so far as it is expressed to apply for general or residual purposes of any of those Acts or for the purposes of this section.

PART 3

GENERAL

32   Minor and consequential amendments and repeals

    (1) Schedule 2 (minor and consequential amendments and repeals) shall have effect.

附錄二　英國《國民緊急應變法（2004）》

Changes to legislation: Civil Contingencies Act 2004 is up to date with all changes known to be in force on or before
21 August 2022. There are changes that may be brought into force at a future date. Changes that have been made
appear in the content and are referenced with annotations. (See end of Document for details) View outstanding changes

(2) The enactments listed in Schedule 3 are hereby repealed or revoked to the extent specified.

Commencement Information

I11 S. 32 partly in force; s. 32 not in force at Royal Assent see s. 34; s. 32(1)(2) in force for specified purposes at 10.12.2004 and s. 32(1) in force for further specified purposes at 19.1.2005 by S.I. 2004/3281, **art. 2**; s. 32 in force for further specified purposes at 1.4.2005 by S.I. 2005/772, **art. 2(d)**; s. 32 in force for further specified purposes at 14.11.2005 by S.I. 2005/2040, **art. 3(n)**

33 Money

There shall be paid out of money provided by Parliament—

(a) any expenditure incurred by a Minister of the Crown in connection with this Act, and

(b) any increase attributable to this Act in the sums payable under any other enactment out of money provided by Parliament.

34 Commencement

(1) The preceding provisions of this Act shall come into force in accordance with provision made by a Minister of the Crown by order.

(2) But the following provisions of this Act shall come into force in accordance with provision made by the Scottish Ministers by order—

(a) section 1(4) in so far as it relates to the Scottish Ministers,

(b) sections 2(4) and (6), 3(2), 4(3) and (7), 5(2) and (5), 6(2) and (5), 8, 9(2), 11, 13(2), 14(2), 17(3) and (5), and

(c) a provision of section 2, 3, 4, 5, 6, 9, 13 or 17 in so far as it relates to a provision specified in paragraph (b) above.

(3) An order under subsection (1) or (2)—

(a) may make provision generally or for specific purposes only,

(b) may make different provision for different purposes,

(c) may make incidental, consequential or transitional provision, and

(d) shall be made by statutory instrument.

Subordinate Legislation Made

P1 S. 34(1)(3) power partly exercised: different dates appointed for specified provisions and purposes by {S.I. 2004/3281}, art. 2; 1.4.2005 appointed for especified provisions and purposes by {S.I. 2005/772}, art. 2; different dates appointed for specified provisions and purposes by {S.I. 2005/2040}, arts. 2-4

P2 S. 34(2)(3) power partly exercised: different dates appointed for specified provisions and purposes by {S.S.I. 2005/493}, arts. 3-5

35 Extent

(1) This Act extends to—

35

附錄二 英國《國民緊急應變法 (2004)》

Changes to legislation: Civil Contingencies Act 2004 is up to date with all changes known to be in force on or before
21 August 2022. There are changes that may be brought into force at a future date. Changes that have been made
appear in the content and are referenced with annotations. (See end of Document for details) View outstanding changes

(a)   England and Wales,

(b)   Scotland, and

(c)   Northern Ireland.

(2) But where this Act amends or repeals an enactment or a provision of an enactment,
the amendment or repeal has the same extent as the enactment or provision.

36   Short title

This Act may be cited as the Civil Contingencies Act 2004.

Changes to legislation: Civil Contingencies Act 2004 *is up to date with all changes known to be in force on or before*
21 August 2022. There are changes that may be brought into force at a future date. Changes that have been made
appear in the content and are referenced with annotations. (See end of Document for details) View outstanding changes

SCHEDULES

SCHEDULE 1   Part 1

CATEGORY 1 AND 2 RESPONDERS

Modifications etc. (not altering text)
C3   Sch. 1 modified (31.12.2020) by The Railway (Licensing of Railway Undertakings) (Amendment etc.)
(EU Exit) Regulations 2019 (S.I. 2019/700), regs. 1(2), **41**; 2020 c. 1, Sch. 5 para. 1(1)

PART 1

CATEGORY 1 RESPONDERS: GENERAL

Modifications etc. (not altering text)
C4   Sch. 1 Pt. 1 modified (temp.) (W.) (24.5.2018 until the repeal of 2006 c. 41, s. 25 by 2012 c. 7, s. 179
comes into force) by The Welsh Ministers (Transfer of Functions) Order 2018 (S.I. 2018/644), arts. 1(1),
47(2)

Local authorities

1   In relation to England—
             (a)   a county council,
             (b)   a district council,
             (c)   a London borough council,
             (d)   the Common Council of the City of London, and
             (e)   the Council of the Isles of Scilly.
[^F72^1A   The Greater London Authority.]

Textual Amendments
F72   Sch. 1 para. 1A inserted (6.5.2011) by The Civil Contingencies Act 2004 (Amendment of List of
Responders) Order 2011 (S.I. 2011/1223), arts. 1, 2

^F73^2   . . . .

Textual Amendments
F73   Sch. 1 para. 2 omitted (24.5.2018) by virtue of The Welsh Ministers (Transfer of Functions) Order 2018
(S.I. 2018/644), arts. 1(1), **41(18)(a)**

Emergency services

3   (1) A chief officer of police within the meaning of section 101(1) of the Police Act 1996 (c. 16).

(2) The Chief Constable of the Police Service of Northern Ireland.

(3) The Chief Constable of the British Transport Police Force.

4   A fire and rescue authority [^{F74}in England,] within the meaning of section 1 of the Fire and Rescue Services Act 2004 (c. 21).

Textual Amendments

F74   Words in Sch. 1 para. 4 inserted (24.5.2018) by The Welsh Ministers (Transfer of Functions) Order 2018 (S.I. 2018/644), arts. 1(1), **41(18)(b)**

Health

[^{F75}4A   [^{F76}NHS England].]

Textual Amendments

F75   Sch. 1 para. 4A inserted (1.4.2013) by Health and Social Care Act 2012 (c. 7), s. 306(4), **Sch. 5 para. 132(2)(a)**; S.I. 2013/160, art. 2(2) (with arts. 7-9)

F76   Words in Sch. 1 substituted (1.7.2022) by Health and Care Act 2022 (c. 31), s. 186(6), Sch. 1 para. 1(1)**(2)**; S.I. 2022/734, reg. 2(a), Sch. (with regs. 13, 29, 30)

[^{F77}4B   An integrated care board established under section 14Z25 of the National Health Service Act 2006.]

Textual Amendments

F77   Sch. 1 para. 4B inserted (1.7.2022) by Health and Care Act 2022 (c. 31), s. 186(6), **Sch. 4 para. 80(2)**; S.I. 2022/734, reg. 2(a), Sch. (with regs. 13, 29, 30)

^{F78}5   . . . .

Textual Amendments

F78   Sch. 1 para. 5 omitted (24.5.2018) by virtue of The Welsh Ministers (Transfer of Functions) Order 2018 (S.I. 2018/644), arts. 1(1), **41(18)(c)**

[^{F79}6   An NHS foundation trust within the meaning of section 30 of the National Health Service Act 2006 if, and in so far as, it has the function of providing—

(a)   ambulance services, or

(b)   hospital accommodation and services in relation to accidents and emergencies.]

Changes to legislation: Civil Contingencies Act 2004 is up to date with all changes known to be in force on or before 21 August 2022. There are changes that may be brought into force at a future date. Changes that have been made appear in the content and are referenced with annotations. (See end of Document for details) View outstanding changes

Textual Amendments

F79 Sch. 1 para. 6 substituted (1.4.2009) by The Civil Contingencies Act 2004 (Amendment of List of Responders) Order 2008 (S.I. 2008/3012), **art. 2**

^{F80}7 . . . .

Textual Amendments

F80 Sch. 1 para. 7 omitted (1.4.2013) by virtue of Health and Social Care Act 2012 (c. 7), s. 306(4), **Sch. 5 para. 132(2)(b)**; S.I. 2013/160, art. 2(2) (with arts. 7-9)

^{F81}8 . . . .

Textual Amendments

F81 Sch. 1 para. 8 omitted (24.5.2018) by virtue of The Welsh Ministers (Transfer of Functions) Order 2018 (S.I. 2018/644), arts. 1(1), **41(18)(d)**

[^{F82}9 The Secretary of State, in so far as the functions of the Secretary of State include responding to emergencies by virtue of —

   (a)   the Secretary of State's functions under section 2A of the National Health Service Act 2006,

   (b)   the Secretary of State's functions under section 58 of the Health and Social Care Act 2012 in so far as it applies in relation to Wales or Scotland, or

   (c)   arrangements made by the Welsh Ministers or Scottish Ministers under which the Secretary of State exercises on their behalf functions in relation to protecting the public in Wales or Scotland from disease or other dangers to health.]

Textual Amendments

F82 Sch. 1 para. 9 substituted (1.4.2013) by Health and Social Care Act 2012 (c. 7), s. 306(4), **Sch. 7 para. 16**; S.I. 2013/160, art. 2(2) (with arts. 7-9)

10   A port health authority [^{F83}in England] constituted under section 2(4) of the Public Health (Control of Disease) Act 1984 (c. 22).

Textual Amendments

F83 Words in Sch. 1 para. 10 inserted (24.5.2018) by The Welsh Ministers (Transfer of Functions) Order 2018 (S.I. 2018/644), arts. 1(1), **41(18)(e)**

Miscellaneous

11   The Environment Agency.

12   The Secretary of State, in so far as his functions include responding to maritime and coastal emergencies (excluding the investigation of accidents).

Changes to legislation: Civil Contingencies Act 2004 is up to date with all changes known to be in force on or before
21 August 2022. There are changes that may be brought into force at a future date. Changes that have been made
appear in the content and are referenced with annotations. (See end of Document for details) View outstanding changes

F84 12A ....

Textual Amendments

F84 Sch. 1 para. 12A omitted (24.5.2018) by virtue of The Welsh Ministers (Transfer of Functions) Order 2018 (S.I. 2018/644), arts. 1(1), **41(18)(f)**

PART 2

CATEGORY 1 RESPONDERS: SCOTLAND

Local authorities

13   A council constituted under section 2 of the Local Government etc. (Scotland) Act 1994 (c. 39).

Emergency services

[F85 14.   The chief constable of the Police Service of Scotland.]

Textual Amendments

F85 Sch. 1 para. 14 substituted (S.) (1.4.2013) by The Police and Fire Reform (Scotland) Act 2012 (Consequential Modifications and Savings) Order 2013 (S.S.I. 2013/119), art. 1, **Sch. 3 para. 1(a)** (with s. 179(5)(b))

[F86 15.   The Scottish Fire and Rescue Service.]

Textual Amendments

F86 Sch. 1 para. 15 substituted (S.) (1.4.2013) by The Police and Fire Reform (Scotland) Act 2012 (Consequential Modifications and Savings) Order 2013 (S.S.I. 2013/119), art. 1, **Sch. 3 para. 1(b)**

16   The Scottish Ambulance Service Board.

Health

17   A Health Board constituted under section 2 of the National Health Service (Scotland) Act 1978 (c. 29).

[F87 *Integration authorities*

Textual Amendments

F87 Sch. 1 para. 17A and cross-heading inserted (S.) (17.3.2021) by The Civil Contingencies Act 2004 (Amendment of List of Responders) (Scotland) Order 2021 (S.S.I. 2021/147), arts. 1, **2**

17A.   An integration authority within the meaning of section 59 of the Public Bodies (Joint Working) (Scotland) Act 2014.]

*Changes to legislation: Civil Contingencies Act 2004 is up to date with all changes known to be in force on or before
21 August 2022. There are changes that may be brought into force at a future date. Changes that have been made
appear in the content and are referenced with annotations. (See end of Document for details) View outstanding changes*

Miscellaneous

18   The Scottish Environment Protection Agency.

[F88PART 2A

CATEGORY 1 RESPONDERS: WALES

Textual Amendments

F88   Sch. 1 Pt. 2A inserted (24.5.2018) by The Welsh Ministers (Transfer of Functions) Order 2018 (S.I. 2018/644), arts. 1(1), **41(19)**

Local authorities

18A.   (1) A county council in Wales.

(2) A county borough council.

Emergency services

18B.   A fire and rescue authority in Wales within the meaning of section 1 of the Fire and Rescue Services Act 2004.

Health

18C.   A National Health Service trust established under section 18 of the National Health Service (Wales) Act 2006 if, and so far as, it has the function of providing—

(a)   ambulance services,

(b)   hospital accommodation and services in relation to accidents and emergencies, or

(c)   services in relation to public health.

18D.   A Local Health Board established under section 11 of the National Health Service (Wales) Act 2006.

Environment

18E.   The Natural Resources Body for Wales.

Port Health Authorities

18F.   A port health authority in Wales constituted under section 2(4) of the Public Health (Control of Disease) Act 1984.]

PART 3

CATEGORY 2 RESPONDERS: GENERAL

Utilities

19   (1) A person holding a licence of a kind specified in sub-paragraph (2) and granted under section 6 of the Electricity Act 1989 (c. 29).

(2) Those licences are—

    (a)   a transmission licence,

    (b)   a distribution licence, and

    (c)   an interconnector licence.

(3) Expressions used in this paragraph and in the Electricity Act 1989 shall have the same meaning in this paragraph as in that Act.

20   (1) A person holding a licence of a kind specified in sub-paragraph (2).

(2) Those licences are—

    (a)   a licence under section 7 of the Gas Act 1986 (c. 44), and

    (b)   a licence under section 7ZA of that Act.

21   A water undertaker or sewerage undertaker [F89for an area wholly or mainly in England] appointed under section 6 of the Water Industry Act 1991 (c. 56).

Textual Amendments

F89 Words in Sch. 1 para. 21 inserted (24.5.2018) by The Welsh Ministers (Transfer of Functions) Order 2018 (S.I. 2018/644), arts. 1(1), **41(20)**

---

22   (1) A person who provides a public electronic communications network which makes telephone services available (whether for spoken communication or for the transmission of data).

(2) In sub-paragraph (1)—

    (a)   the reference to provision of a network shall be construed in accordance with section 32(4)(a) and (b) of the Communications Act 2003 (c. 21), and

    (b)   "public electronic communications network" shall have the meaning given by sections 32(1) and 151(1) of that Act.

Transport

23   A person who holds a licence under section 8 of the Railways Act 1993 (c. 43) (operation of railway assets) in so far as the licence relates to activity in Great Britain.

[F9024   A person who provides services in connection with railways in Great Britain and who holds—

    (a)   a railway undertaking licence granted pursuant to the Railway (Licensing of Railway Undertakings) Regulations 2005; or

    (b)   a relevant European licence, within the meaning of section 6(2) of the Railways Act 1993.]

Changes to legislation: Civil Contingencies Act 2004 is up to date with all changes known to be in force on or before 21 August 2022. There are changes that may be brought into force at a future date. Changes that have been made appear in the content and are referenced with annotations. (See end of Document for details) View outstanding changes

Textual Amendments

F90 Sch. 1 para. 24 substituted (31.1.2022 at 11.00 p.m.) by The Railway (Licensing of Railway Undertakings) (Amendment) Regulations 2021 (S.I. 2021/1105), regs. 1(3), **11**

25   (1) Transport for London.

        (2) London Underground Limited (being a subsidiary of Transport for London).

26   An airport operator, within the meaning of section 82(1) of the Airports Act 1986 (c. 31), in Great Britain.

[F91 26A   A person who, for the purposes of Part 1 of the Civil Aviation Act 2012, is an operator of an airport area that consists of or forms part of an airport in Great Britain.]

Textual Amendments

F91 Sch. 1 para. 26A inserted (6.4.2013) by Civil Aviation Act 2012 (c. 19), s. 110(1), **Sch. 9 para. 16(2)** (with Sch. 10 para. 1217); S.I. 2013/589, art. 2(3)

27   A harbour authority, within the meaning of section 46(1) of the Aviation and Maritime Security Act 1990 (c. 31), in Great Britain.

28 [F92 (1)] The Secretary of State, in so far as his functions relate to matters for which he is responsible by virtue of section 1 of the Highways Act 1980 (c. 66) (highway authorities).

   [F93 (2) A strategic highways company for the time being appointed under Part 1 of the Infrastructure Act 2015.]

Textual Amendments

F92 Sch. 1 para. 28 renumbered as Sch. 1 para. 28(1) (5.3.2015) by Infrastructure Act 2015 (c. 7), s. 57(1), **Sch. 1 para. 152(a)**; S.I. 2015/481, reg. 2(a)

F93 Sch. 1 para. 28(2) inserted (5.3.2015) by Infrastructure Act 2015 (c. 7), s. 57(1), **Sch. 1 para. 152(b)**; S.I. 2015/481, reg. 2(a)

Health and safety

29   The Health and Safety Executive.

[F94 Health]

Textual Amendments

F94 Sch. 1 para. 29A and preceding cross-heading inserted (14.11.2005) by The Civil Contingencies Act 2004 (Amendment of List of Responders) Order 2005 (S.I. 2005/2043), **art. 2(b)**

F95 29ZA   . . . .

Changes to legislation: *Civil Contingencies Act 2004 is up to date with all changes known to be in force on or before 21 August 2022. There are changes that may be brought into force at a future date. Changes that have been made appear in the content and are referenced with annotations. (See end of Document for details) View outstanding changes*

Textual Amendments

F95 Sch. 1 para. 29ZA omitted (1.7.2022) by virtue of Health and Care Act 2022 (c. 31), s. 186(6), **Sch. 4 para. 80(3)**; S.I. 2022/734, reg. 2(a), Sch. (with regs. 13, 29, 30)

[F96] **29A** ....

Textual Amendments

F96 Sch. 1 para. 29A omitted (1.4.2013) by virtue of Health and Social Care Act 2012 (c. 7), s. 306(4), **Sch. 5 para. 132(3)(b)**; S.I. 2013/160, art. 2(2) (with arts. 7-9)

[F97 *Miscellaneous*

Textual Amendments

F97 Sch. 1 para. 29B and preceding cross-heading inserted (1.4.2014) by Energy Act 2013 (c. 32), s. 156(1), **Sch. 12 para. 81**; S.I. 2014/251, art. 4

29B   The Office for Nuclear Regulation.]

PART 4

CATEGORY 2 RESPONDERS: SCOTLAND

Utilities

30   (1) A person holding a licence of a kind specified in sub-paragraph (2) and granted under the Electricity Act 1989 (c. 29), in so far as the activity under the licence is undertaken in Scotland.

   (2) Those licences are—

      (a)   a transmission licence,

      (b)   a distribution licence, and

      (c)   an interconnector licence.

   (3) Expressions used in this paragraph and in the Electricity Act 1989 shall have the same meaning in this paragraph as in that Act.

31   (1) A person holding a licence of a kind specified in sub-paragraph (2), in so far as the activity under the licence is undertaken in Scotland.

   (2) Those licences are—

      (a)   a licence under section 7 of the Gas Act 1986 (c. 44), and

      (b)   a licence under section 7ZA of that Act.

32   Scottish Water, established by section 20 of, and Schedule 3 to, the Water Industry (Scotland) Act 2002 (asp 3).

Changes to legislation: Civil Contingencies Act 2004 is up to date with all changes known to be in force on or before
21 August 2022. There are changes that may be brought into force at a future date. Changes that have been made
appear in the content and are referenced with annotations. (See end of Document for details) View outstanding changes

33   (1) A person who provides a public electronic communications network which makes telephone services available (whether for spoken communication or for the transmission of data) in so far as the services are made available in Scotland.

(2) In sub-paragraph (1)—

(a)   the reference to provision of a network shall be construed in accordance with section 32(4)(a) and (b) of the Communications Act 2003 (c. 21), and

(b)   "public electronic communications network" shall have the meaning given by sections 32(1) and 151(1) of that Act.

Transport

34   A person who holds a licence to operate railway assets under section 8 of the Railways Act 1993 (c. 43) in so far as such operation takes place in Scotland.

[F98 35   A person who provides services in connection with railways, in so far as such services are provided in Scotland, and who holds a railway undertaking licence granted pursuant to the Railway (Licensing of Railway Undertakings) Regulations 2005.]

Textual Amendments
  F98   Sch. 1 para. 35 substituted (31.12.2020) by The Railway (Licensing of Railway Undertakings) (Amendment etc.) (EU Exit) Regulations 2019 (S.I. 2019/700), regs. 1(2), **24(b)**; 2020 c. 1, Sch. 5 para. 1(1)

36   An airport operator within the meaning of section 82(1) of the Airports Act 1986 (c. 31) in so far as it has responsibility for the management of an airport in Scotland.

[F99 36A   A person who, for the purposes of Part 1 of the Civil Aviation Act 2012, is an operator of an airport area that consists of or forms part of an airport in Scotland.]

Textual Amendments
  F99   Sch. 1 para. 36A inserted (6.4.2013) by Civil Aviation Act 2012 (c. 19), s. 110(1), **Sch. 9 para. 16(3)** (with Sch. 10 para. 1217); S.I. 2013/589, art. 2(3)

37   A harbour authority, within the meaning of section 46(1) of the Aviation and Maritime Security Act 1990 (c. 31) in so far as it has functions in relation to improving, maintaining and managing a harbour in Scotland.

Health

38   The Common Services Agency established by section 10 of the National Health Service (Scotland) Act 1978 (c. 29).

[F100 38A.   Public Health Scotland constituted by the Public Health Scotland Order 2019.]

Textual Amendments
  F100   Sch. 1 para. 38A inserted (S.) (1.4.2020) by The Public Health Scotland Order 2019 (S.S.I. 2019/336), art. 1(3)(b), **sch. 2 para. 4(2)** (with art. 4(4)(5))

Civil Contingencies Act 2004 (c. 36)
SCHEDULE 2 – Minor and Consequential Amendments and Repeals
Document Generated: 2022-08-21

45

Changes to legislation: Civil Contingencies Act 2004 is up to date with all changes known to be in force on or before 21 August 2022. There are changes that may be brought into force at a future date. Changes that have been made appear in the content and are referenced with annotations. (See end of Document for details) View outstanding changes

[F101PART 5

CATEGORY 2 RESPONDERS: WALES

Textual Amendments

F101 Sch. 1 Pt. 5 inserted (24.5.2018) by The Welsh Ministers (Transfer of Functions) Order 2018 (S.I. 2018/644), arts. 1(1), **41(21)**

Utilities

39. A water undertaker or sewerage undertaker appointed under section 6 of the Water Industry Act 1991 for an area wholly or mainly in Wales.

Transport

40. The Welsh Ministers, in so far as their functions relate to matters for which they are responsible by virtue of section 1 of the Highways Act 1980.]

SCHEDULE 2

Section 32

MINOR AND CONSEQUENTIAL AMENDMENTS AND REPEALS

PART 1

AMENDMENTS AND REPEALS CONSEQUENTIAL ON PART 1

Civil Defence Act 1939 (c. 31)

1 The Civil Defence Act 1939 shall cease to have effect.

Civil Defence Act (Northern Ireland) 1939 (c. 15 (N.I.))

2 The Civil Defence Act (Northern Ireland) 1939 shall cease to have effect.

Civil Defence Act 1948 (c. 5)

3 The Civil Defence Act 1948 shall cease to have effect.

Commencement Information

I12 Sch. 2 para. 3 partly in force; Sch. 2 para. 3 not in force at Royal Assent see s. 34; Sch. 2 para. 3 in force for specified purposes at 1.4.2005 by S.I. 2005/772, **art. 2(a)**

Civil Defence Act (Northern Ireland) 1950 (c. 11 (N.I.))

4 The Civil Defence Act (Northern Ireland) 1950 shall cease to have effect.

46

Civil Contingencies Act 2004 (c. 36)
SCHEDULE 2 – Minor and Consequential Amendments and Repeals
Document Generated: 2022-08-21

Changes to legislation: Civil Contingencies Act 2004 is up to date with all changes known to be in force on or before
21 August 2022. There are changes that may be brought into force at a future date. Changes that have been made
appear in the content and are referenced with annotations. (See end of Document for details) View outstanding changes

Defence Contracts Act 1958 (c. 38)

5   In section 6(1) of the Defence Contracts Act 1958 (interpretation, &c.), in the definition of "defence materials" omit paragraph (b).

Public Expenditure and Receipts Act 1968 (c. 14)

6   Section 4 of the Public Expenditure and Receipts Act 1968 (compensation to civil defence employees for loss of employment, &c.) shall cease to have effect.

Local Government Act 1972 (c. 70)

7   In section 138 of the Local Government Act 1972 (emergency powers)—
   (a)   subsection (1A) shall cease to have effect, and
   (b)   in subsection (3) for "subsections (1) and (1A) above" substitute " subsection (1) above ".

Civil Protection in Peacetime Act 1986 (c. 22)

8   The Civil Protection in Peacetime Act 1986 shall cease to have effect.

Road Traffic Act 1988 (c. 52)

9   In section 65A(5) of the Road Traffic Act 1988 (light passenger vehicles and motor cycles not to be sold without EC certificate of conformity) omit paragraph (c).

Metropolitan County Fire and Rescue Authorities

10   (1) The bodies established by section 26 of the Local Government Act 1985 (c. 51) and known as metropolitan county fire and civil defence authorities shall be known instead as metropolitan county fire and rescue authorities.

   (2) So far as necessary or appropriate in consequence of sub-paragraph (1), a reference in an enactment, instrument, agreement or other document to a metropolitan county fire and civil defence authority shall be treated as a reference to a metropolitan county fire and rescue authority.

   (3) In the following provisions for "(fire services, civil defence and transport)" substitute " (fire and rescue services and transport) "
      (a)   F102 . . . .
      (b)   sections 21(1)(i), 39(1)(g), 67(3)(k) and 152(2)(i) of the Local Government and Housing Act 1989 (c. 42),
      (c)   section 1(10)(d) of the Local Government (Overseas Assistance) Act 1993 (c. 25),
      (d)   paragraph 19 of Schedule 1 to the Freedom of Information Act 2000 (c. 36), and
      (e)   sections 23(1)(k) and 33(1)(j) of the Local Government Act 2003 (c. 26).

Civil Contingencies Act 2004 (c. 36)
SCHEDULE 2 – Minor and Consequential Amendments and Repeals
Document Generated: 2022-08-21

47

Changes to legislation: Civil Contingencies Act 2004 is up to date with all changes known to be in force on or before
21 August 2022. There are changes that may be brought into force at a future date. Changes that have been made
appear in the content and are referenced with annotations. (See end of Document for details) View outstanding changes

附錄二 英國《國民緊急應變法（2004）》

Textual Amendments

F102 Sch. 2 para. 10(3)(a) repealed (E.W.S.) (5.4.2011) by Equality Act 2010 (c. 15), Sch. 27 Pt. 1A (as
inserted (4.4.2011) by The Equality Act 2010 (Public Authorities and Consequential and Supplementary
Amendments) Order 2011 (S.I. 2011/1060), arts. 1(2), 3(3)(a), **Sch. 3**); S.I. 2011/1066, **art. 2(e)(h)**

PART 2

AMENDMENTS AND REPEALS CONSEQUENTIAL ON PART 2

Emergency Powers Act 1920 (c. 55)

11   The Emergency Powers Act 1920 shall cease to have effect.

Emergency Powers Act (Northern Ireland) 1926 (c. 8)

12   The Emergency Powers Act (Northern Ireland) 1926 shall cease to have effect.

Northern Ireland Act 1998 (c. 47)

13   In paragraph 14 of Schedule 3 to the Northern Ireland Act 1998 (reserved matters)
for "the Emergency Powers Act (Northern Ireland) 1926" substitute " Part 2 of the
Civil Contingencies Act 2004 ".

PART 3

MINOR AMENDMENTS

Energy Act 1976 (c. 76)

14   After sections 1 to 4 of the Energy Act 1976 (powers to control production and
supply of fuel, &c.) insert—

"5 Sections 1 to 4: territorial application

"5   "5 Sections 1 to 4: territorial application

(1) A power under sections 1 to 4 may be exercised in relation to anything which
is wholly or partly situated in, or to activity wholly or partly in—

    (a)   the United Kingdom,

    (b)   the territorial sea of the United Kingdom, or

    (c)   an area designated under the Continental Shelf Act 1964 (c. 29).

(2) Subsection (1) is without prejudice to section 2(2)(b)."

Highways Act 1980 (c. 66)

15   15 (1) At the end of section 90H(2) of the Highways Act 1980 (traffic calming works
regulations) add—

48   *Civil Contingencies Act 2004 (c. 36)*
SCHEDULE 2 – Minor and Consequential Amendments and Repeals
Document Generated: 2022-08-21

Changes to legislation: *Civil Contingencies Act 2004 is up to date with all changes known to be in force on or before 21 August 2022. There are changes that may be brought into force at a future date. Changes that have been made appear in the content and are referenced with annotations. (See end of Document for details) View outstanding changes*

"(d)   provide that, in such cases or circumstances as the regulations may specify, works may be constructed or removed only with the consent of a police officer of such class as the regulations may specify."

(2) In section 329(1) of that Act (interpretation) for the definition of "traffic calming works" substitute—

""traffic calming works", in relation to a highway, means works affecting the movement of vehicular or other traffic for the purpose of—

    (a) promoting safety (including avoiding or reducing, or reducing the likelihood of, danger connected with terrorism within the meaning of section 1 of the Terrorism Act 2000 (c. 11)), or

    (b) preserving or improving the environment through which the highway runs;".

Road Traffic Regulation Act 1984 (c. 27)

16   (1) The Road Traffic Regulation Act 1984 shall be amended as follows.

(2) In Part 2 (traffic regulation: special cases) after section 22B insert—

"22C Terrorism

"22C "22C Terrorism

(1) An order may be made under section 1(1)(a) for the purpose of avoiding or reducing, or reducing the likelihood of, danger connected with terrorism (for which purpose the reference to persons or other traffic using the road shall be treated as including a reference to persons or property on or near the road).

(2) An order may be made under section 1(1)(b) for the purpose of preventing or reducing damage connected with terrorism.

(3) An order under section 6 made for a purpose mentioned in section 1(1)(a) or (b) may be made for that purpose as qualified by subsection (1) or (2) above.

(4) An order may be made under section 14(1)(b) for a purpose relating to danger or damage connected with terrorism.

(5) A notice may be issued under section 14(2)(b) for a purpose relating to danger or damage connected with terrorism.

(6) In this section "terrorism" has the meaning given by section 1 of the Terrorism Act 2000 (c. 11).

(7) In Scotland an order made, or notice issued, by virtue of this section is to be made or issued not by the traffic authority, if the traffic authority is the Scottish Ministers, but by the Secretary of State.

(8) In Wales an order made, or notice issued, by virtue of this section may be made or issued only with the consent of the Secretary of State if the traffic authority is the National Assembly for Wales.

Civil Contingencies Act 2004 (c. 36)
SCHEDULE 2 – Minor and Consequential Amendments and Repeals
Document Generated: 2022-08-21

49

22D Section 22C: supplemental

22D   22D Section 22C: supplemental

> (1) An order may be made by virtue of section 22C only on the recommendation of the chief officer of police for the area to which the order relates.
>
> (2) The following shall not apply in relation to an order made by virtue of section 22C—
>> (a)   section 3,
>> (b)   section 6(5),
>> (c)   the words in section 14(4) from "but" to the end,
>> (d)   section 121B, and
>> (e)   paragraph 13(1)(a) of Schedule 9.
>
> (3) Sections 92 and 94 shall apply in relation to an order under section 14 made by virtue of section 22C as they apply in relation to an order under section 1 or 6.
>
> (4) An order made by virtue of section 22C, or an authorisation or requirement by virtue of subsection (3) above, may authorise the undertaking of works for the purpose of, or for a purpose ancillary to, another provision of the order, authorisation or requirement.
>
> (5) An order made by virtue of section 22C may—
>> (a)   enable a constable to direct that a provision of the order shall (to such extent as the constable may specify) be commenced, suspended or revived;
>> (b)   confer a discretion on a constable;
>> (c)   make provision conferring a power on a constable in relation to the placing of structures or signs (which may, in particular, apply a provision of this Act with or without modifications)."

(3) In section 67 (traffic signs: emergencies &c.) after subsection (1) insert—

"(1A) In subsection (1)—
> (a)   "extraordinary circumstances" includes terrorism or the prospect of terrorism within the meaning of section 1 of the Terrorism Act 2000 (c. 11), and
> (b)   the reference to 7 days shall, in the application of the subsection in connection with terrorism or the prospect of terrorism, be taken as a reference to 28 days;

but this subsection does not apply to a power under subsection (1) in so far as exercisable by a traffic officer by virtue of section 7 of the Traffic Management Act 2004 (c. 18)."

(4) In Schedule 9 (reserve powers of Secretary of State, Scottish Ministers and National Assembly for Wales)—
> (a)   in paragraph 1, after "sections 1, 6, 9," insert " 14 (in so far as the power under that section is exercisable by virtue of section 22C), ", and—
> (b)   after paragraph 12 insert—

50

Civil Contingencies Act 2004 (c. 36)
SCHEDULE 2 – Minor and Consequential Amendments and Repeals
Document Generated: 2022-08-21

Changes to legislation: Civil Contingencies Act 2004 is up to date with all changes known to be in force on or before 21 August 2022. There are changes that may be brought into force at a future date. Changes that have been made appear in the content and are referenced with annotations. (See end of Document for details) View outstanding changes

"12A   Article 2 of the Scotland Act 1998 (Transfer of Functions to the Scottish Ministers etc.) Order 1999 (SI 1999/1750) shall not apply to a provision of this Schedule in so far as it relates to the exercise of a power under this Act by virtue of section 22C.

12B   A power conferred upon the Secretary of State by this Schedule shall, in so far as it relates to the exercise of a power under this Act by virtue of section 22C, be exercisable in relation to Wales by the National Assembly for Wales with the consent of the Secretary of State.".

Roads (Scotland) Act 1984 (c. 54)

17   (1) After section 39B of the Roads (Scotland) Act 1984 (traffic calming works regulations) insert—

"39BA Prescribing of works for anti-terrorism purposes

"39BA "39BA Prescribing of works for anti-terrorism purposes

(1) Where—

(a)   the construction of any traffic calming works is for the purpose of avoiding or reducing, or reducing the likelihood of, danger connected with terrorism within the meaning of section 1 of the Terrorism Act 2000, and

(b)   the function of constructing those works would, but for this section, be exercisable by the Scottish Ministers,

that function shall instead be exercisable by the Secretary of State.

(2) The power to make regulations under section 39B of this Act—

(a)   for the purpose of, or in connection with, avoiding or reducing, or reducing the likelihood of, danger connected with terrorism within the meaning of section 1 of the Terrorism Act 2000, and

(b)   which would, but for this section, be exercisable by the Scottish Ministers,

shall instead be exercisable by the Secretary of State.

(3) Regulations under section 39B of this Act may, if they are made by virtue of subsection (2) above, provide that, in such circumstances as the regulations may specify, works may be constructed or removed only with the consent of a police officer of such class as the regulations may specify."

(2) In section 40 of that Act (interpretation of sections 36 to 39C) for the definition of "traffic calming works" substitute—

""traffic calming works", in relation to a road, means works affecting the movement of vehicular or other traffic for the purpose of—

(a) promoting safety (including avoiding or reducing, or reducing the likelihood of, danger connected with terrorism within the meaning of section 1 of the Terrorism Act 2000 (c. 11)), or

(b) preserving or improving the environment through which the road runs."

附錄二 英國《國民緊急應變法（2004）》

SCHEDULE 3   Section 32

REPEALS AND REVOCATIONS

Commencement Information

I13   Sch. 3 partly in force; Sch. 3 not in force at Royal Assent see s. 34; Sch. 3 in force for specified purposes
at 10.12.2004 by S.I. 2004/3281, **art. 2(2)**; Sch. 3 in force for further specified purposes at 1.4.2005 by
S.I. 2005/772, **art. 2(c)**; Sch. 3 in force for further specified purposes at 14.11.2005 by S.I. 2005/2040,
art. 3(r)

Short title and chapter	*Repeal or revocation*
The Emergency Powers Act 1920 (c. 55).	The whole Act.
The Emergency Powers Act (Northern Ireland) 1926 (c. 8).	The whole Act.
The Air-Raid Precautions Act (Northern Ireland) 1938 (c. 26 (N.I.)).	The whole Act.
The Civil Defence Act 1939 (c. 31).	The whole Act.
The Civil Defence Act (Northern Ireland) 1939 (c. 15 (N.I.)).	The whole Act.
The Civil Defence Act 1948 (c. 5).	The whole Act.
The Civil Defence Act (Northern Ireland) 1950 (c. 11 (N.I.)).	The whole Act.
The Criminal Justice Act (Northern Ireland) 1953 (c. 14 (N.I.)).	In Schedule 2, the entry relating to the Civil Defence Act (Northern Ireland) 1950.
The Civil Defence (Armed Forces) Act 1954 (c. 66).	The whole Act.
The Defence Contracts Act 1958 (c. 38).	In section 6(1), in the definition of "defence materials", paragraph (b).
The Town and Country Planning (Scotland) Act 1959 (c. 70).	In paragraph 2 of Schedule 4, the entry relating to the Civil Defence Act 1948.
The Emergency Powers Act 1964 (c. 38).	Section 1.
The Lands Tribunal and Compensation Act (Northern Ireland) 1964 (c. 29 (N.I.)).	In Schedule 1, the entry relating to the Civil Defence Act (Northern Ireland) 1939.
The Emergency Powers (Amendment) Act (Northern Ireland) 1964 (c. 34 (N.I.)).	The whole Act.
The Police (Scotland) Act 1967 (c. 77).	In Schedule 4, the entry relating to the Civil Defence Act 1948.
The Public Expenditure and Receipts Act 1968 (c. 14).	Section 4.
The Land Charges Act 1972 (c. 61).	In Schedule 2, paragraph 1(f).
The Local Government Act 1972 (c. 70).	Section 138(1A).

Changes to legislation: Civil Contingencies Act 2004 is up to date with all changes known to be in force on or before 21 August 2022. There are changes that may be brought into force at a future date. Changes that have been made appear in the content and are referenced with annotations. (See end of Document for details) View outstanding changes

The Drainage (Northern Ireland) Order 1973 (S.I. 1973/69 (N.I. 1)).	In Schedule 8, paragraphs 3 and 4.
The Statute Law (Repeals) Act 1976 (c. 16).	In Schedule 2, in Part II, the entry relating to the Civil Defence Act 1939.
The Road Traffic (Northern Ireland) Order 1981 (S.I. 1981/154 (N.I. 1)).	Article 31G(5)(c).
The Civil Aviation Act 1982 (c. 16).	In Schedule 2, paragraph 2.
The Criminal Justice Act 1982 (c. 48).	Section 41.
The Police and Criminal Evidence Act 1984 (c. 60).	In Schedule 2, the entry relating to section 2 of the Emergency Powers Act 1920.
The Fines and Penalties (Northern Ireland) Order 1984 (S.I. 1984/703 (N.I. 3)).	Article 12.
The Civil Protection in Peacetime Act 1986 (c. 22).	The whole Act.
The Road Traffic Act 1988 (c. 52).	Section 65A(5)(c).
The Water Act 1989 (c. 15).	In Schedule 25, paragraph 1(4).
The Electricity Act 1989 (c. 29).	In Schedule 16, paragraph 1(3) and paragraph 4.
The Police and Criminal Evidence (Northern Ireland) Order 1989 (S.I. 1989/1341 (N.I. 12)).	In Schedule 2, the entry relating to the Emergency Powers Act (Northern Ireland) 1926.
The Local Government Finance Act 1992 (c. 14).	In Schedule 13, paragraph 6.
The Local Government etc. (Scotland) Act 1994 (c. 39).	In Schedule 13, paragraph 24.
The Gas Act 1995 (c. 45).	In Schedule 4, paragraph 2(5).
The Police Act 1997 (c. 50).	In Schedule 9, paragraphs 2 and 17.
The Greater London Authority Act 1999 (c. 29).	Section 330.
The Transport Act 2000 (c. 38).	In Schedule 5, paragraph 3.
The Civil Defence (Grant) Act 2002 (c. 5).	The whole Act.

Changes to legislation:
Civil Contingencies Act 2004 is up to date with all changes known to be in force on or before
21 August 2022. There are changes that may be brought into force at a future date. Changes that
have been made appear in the content and are referenced with annotations.
View outstanding changes

Changes and effects yet to be applied to :
- Sch. 1 para. 5 words omitted by 2012 c. 7 Sch. 14 para. 100

Changes and effects yet to be applied to the whole Act associated Parts and Chapters:
Whole provisions yet to be inserted into this Act (including any effects on those
provisions):
- Sch. 1 para. 11A inserted by 2006 c. 16 Sch. 11 para. 174 (Sch. 11 para. 174 repealed
  (12.1.2010) without ever being in force by 2009 c. 23, Sch. 22 Pt. 8; S.I. 2009/3345,
  art. 2, Sch. para 27(d))

責任編輯　　蘇健偉

書籍設計　　a_kun

書　　名	**香港特區行政長官的緊急立法權研究**
	基於對《緊急情況規例條例》文本的分析
著　　者	朱世海　黃海鵬
出　　版	三聯書店（香港）有限公司
	香港北角英皇道 499 號北角工業大廈 20 樓
	Joint Publishing (H.K.) Co., Ltd.
	20/F., North Point Industrial Building,
	499 King's Road, North Point, Hong Kong
香港發行	香港聯合書刊物流有限公司
	香港新界荃灣德士古道 220-248 號 16 樓
印　　刷	美雅印刷製本有限公司
	香港九龍觀塘榮業街 6 號 4 樓 A 室
版　　次	2022 年 12 月香港第一版第一次印刷
規　　格	大 32 開（140mm × 210 mm）248 面
國際書號	ISBN 978-962-04-5126-3